> By the streams that ever flow,
> By the fragrant winds that blow
> O'er th' Elysian flow'rs,
> By those happy souls who dwell
> In yellow meads of Asphodel,
> Or Amaranthine bow'rs

The Master is a tragic protagonist, then, and one who has sealed away any thought of love in grim memorial of his lost paramour. Yet within little more than a page the Master has cast away the "knot of ash-coloured hair" (12) he once plucked from his lover's crown and has spent the night in the bower of the Crimson Weaver where she "gave of him nepenthe" (13), the Homeric draught that "chases away sorrow"; quite literally an antidepressant. This could be simple expediency to draw the story to a close, but the Master's curt description of his apparently heart-shattering woe is less than convincing; "the woman died" is not a description of all-devouring grief. Perhaps there are other voices who wish to speak to us in this tale.

Our first clue is in the very specific use of asphodel; yes, it is a mourning flower, but in such a Gothic tale are we truly to believe that the gaunt, pale blooms are to be a fond remembrance of love? Persephone, for whom the morbid flowers are an emblem, is not a romantic goddess; she was stolen by Hades and dragged down to the underworld to be his bride but, it could be argued, ultimately performs the role of judge and jailor of the dead far more fastidiously than her husband ever did. Homer repeatedly refers to her as "dread Persephone," beloved of the witch-queen Hekate, and describes her charges not as the "happy souls" of Pope but as "whining and gibbering" spirits that "sweep shadow-like around" before being summoned to give counsel only with offerings of blood. Odysseus tells us (*Odyssey* 11.33–43):

> But when I had besought the tribes of the dead with vows and prayers, I took the sheep and cut their throats over the trench, and the dark blood flowed forth, and lo, the spirits of the dead that be departed gathered them from out of Erebus. Brides and youths unwed, and old men of many and evil days, and tender maidens with grief yet fresh at heart; and many there were, wounded with bronze-shod spears, men slain in fight with their bloody mail about them. And

> these many ghosts flocked together from every side about the trench with a wondrous cry, and pale fear gat hold on me. (Homer 173)

This adds a pallid complexion to the Master's metaphorical mausoleum, the candlelit and flower-strewn chamber less a place of fond mourning than it is an oubliette of tortured howls and flitting shadows. The Master's lover does not rest as easily as he would have us believe.

Our second clue comes close on the heels of the Master's tale when the Apprentice explains:

> By this time we had reached the skirt of a yew-forest, traversed in every direction by narrow paths. The air was moist and heavy, but ever and anon a light wind touched the tree-tops and bowed them, so that the pollen sank in golden veils to the ground. (10)

Yew is an evocative and ill-omened tree, with something of the vampire lingering in its dark branches. It can live to be almost impossibly old (the Fortingall Yew in Perthshire, Scotland, is commonly believed to be 2000 years old, perhaps more); it has a tendency to flourish in graveyards, and almost every part of it (the blood-red fruit being a singular exception) is toxic to both humans and animals. Yet it is not often known that it can also be hallucinogenic. German medical professor A. Kukowka recounts a tale of "gardening under the branches of four yew trees" when he "was overcome by dizziness, nausea, headache and disorientation." He lost his sense of time and began to hallucinate: scenes of vampires and vipers were soon followed by "visions of a paradisiacal realm" (Hageneder 99). Equally, the first-century C.E. Greek physician and pharmacologist Dioscorides claimed that "The yew growing in Narvonia, Spain, has such a power that those who sit or sleep under its shade suffer harm, or in many cases die" (Hageneder 99).

Consider this in light of the experience of the Master and his Apprentice. After long travel and toil, burdened by dark thoughts of death and loss, they pass through a miasmic yew-forest where "pollen sank in golden veils." They then encounter a psychedelic flock of unearthly birds, one of which regards them with "the face of a mannikin" (11), before they emerge into the presence of the Crimson Weaver herself. She is described as a beautiful woman, "perfect of feature," but consumed with a "most tempting sadness" that

DEAD RECKONINGS

A Review of Horror and the Weird in the Arts
Edited by Alex Houstoun and Michael J. Abolafia

No. 21 (Spring 2017)

3   Bestarred with Fainting Flowers .... Daniel Pietersen
    Symbolism and Myth in the Work of R. Murray Gilchrist

10 The "V" Word .... Jose Cruz
    T. E. Grau, *They Don't Come Home Anymore*

14 Shadows with Teeth .... Darrell Schweitzer
    Ellen Datlow, ed. *The Best Horror of the Year, Volume 8*

16 Existential and Ontological Horror .... S. T. Joshi
    Joel Lane, *This Spectacular Darkness: Critical Essays*,
    ed. Mark Valentine and John Howard

21 In the Heliotherapy Ward .... Amber Doll Diaz
    David F. Sandberg, *Lights Out*

25 The Horror in the Card Catalog .... S. T. Joshi
    Darrell Schweitzer and John Ashmead, ed. *Tales from the Miskatonic
    University Library*

30 Southern Discomfort and the Ubiquitous Undead ....
                                                                  Stephanie Graves
    Eric Gary Anderson, Taylor Hagood, and Daniel Cross Turner, ed.
    *Undead Souths: The Gothic and Beyond in Southern Literature and
    Culture*

32 Forever I'm Alone with You .... Jose Cruz
    Lynda E. Rucker, *You'll Know When You Get There*

39 Stranger Things: A Conversation between Bev Vincent and
    Hank Wagner

44 Terrors of the Natural World .... S. T. Joshi
    Richard Gavin, *Sylvan Dread: Tales of Pastoral Darkness*

47 Ramsey's Rant: Remembering Kirby .... Ramsey Campbell

53 Psychosexual Syzygy: Checking in at the Bates Motel ....
                                                                  Gavin Callaghan
    Bates Motel, Seasons 1 through 5

70	Terror for Children ....Taij Devon
	Aric Cushing, *Vampire Boy*
72	The Homely Commonplace and the Unimaginably Deranged: J. G. Ballard's *High Rise* .... Alexander Lugo
80	The Resurgence of Weird Magazines .... Ashley Dioses
83	The Final Work of Mark Fisher .... James Machin
	Mark Fisher, *The Weird and the Eerie*
87	SMASH EVERYTHING! Bobby Rhodes and His *Demons* ...... Nathan Chazan
91	THINKING HORROR: An Exchange with s. j. bagley .... Alex Houstoun
103	Pastiches of Pastiches .... S. T. Joshi
	Brian M. Sammons and Glynn Owen Barrass, ed. *The Children of Gla'aki: A Tribute to Ramsey Campbell's Great Old One*
109	About the Contributors

DEAD RECKONINGS is published by Hippocampus Press, P.O. Box 641, New York, NY 10156 (www.hippocampuspress.com). Copyright © 2017 by Hippocampus Press. Cover art by Jason C. Eckhardt. Cover design by Barbara Briggs Silbert. Hippocampus Press logo by Anastasia Damianakos. Orders and subscriptions should be sent to Hippocampus Press. Contact Alex Houstoun at deadreckoningsjournal@gmail.com for assignments or before submitting a publication for review.

ISSN 1935-6110
ISBN: 978-1-61498-200-5

Bestarred with Fainting Flowers: Symbolism and Myth in the Work of R. Murray Gilchrist

Daniel Pietersen

It is very likely that you have never heard of the more than twenty novels, half-dozen collections of short stories, and four works of nonfiction that Robert Murray Gilchrist (1867–1917) wrote in the forty-nine short years of his life. He languishes in unwarranted obscurity that almost defies the promise he showed in life; he was published in the infamous *Yellow Book* alongside such writers as Henry James, was a correspondent of H. G. Wells, and had a turn of phrase the *Spectator* described as "fantastic beyond description" (*Spectator* 23). His finest works of what we would now call weird horror, where "suicide, madness, drunkenness, disfigurement, dwarfs, hereditary diseases and strange deaths abound" (Bush 5); they sit perfectly between the gloomy corridors of Poe and the awful vistas of Clark Ashton Smith.

Nowadays, however, almost nothing remains. Two editions of his collected short stories, both covering the same ground, are currently in print, but his novels have been consigned to the dusty shelves of reference libraries; there are a mere eight copies of his landmark work, *The Labyrinth*, on public loan in the entire world. Even his entry in the *Oxford Companion to Edwardian Fiction* misstates his date of birth as 1868.

In this essay, written in the centenary of his death, I seek to rehabilitate Gilchrist by looking at one of his key works of weird horror, showing how it acts as a primer for his worldview and where it sits in the canon of horror fiction.

"The Crimson Weaver," first published in Volume 6 of the *Yellow Book* (July 1895), is one of Gilchrist's most obviously weird stories and, as such, is an excellent gateway to the unique voice and denser prose of tales such as "The Stone Dragon" or "The Basilisk." Readers who have explored Lovecraft's less cosmic, less immediately horrifying work, such as the poem "A Garden," in which "There are vines in nooks and crannies, and there's moss about the pool, / And the tangled weedy thicket chokes the arbour dark and cool" (278), or have spent "A Night in Malnéant" with Clark Ashton Smith, whose tale also uses a death that has "broken away from the sequence of time" (59) to tell a similar tale, will find that they are in familiarly unsettling territory. It is a well-constructed tale of physical dissolution and spiritual collapse in the face of forbidden desire; its core narrative of a Master and his Apprentice wandering almost willfully into the "enchanted country" (Gilchrist 10) of an abhuman sorceress, where they forfeit both life and soul, is one that allures and repels in equal measure.

Yet, as effective as the tale is on first reading, we should be wary of taking the weird at face value. Gilchrist himself has the Apprentice recall that the Master had been "telling him of the Platonists" (9), of the concept that the things we experience directly are removed many times over from their true forms, in a subtle nod to the fact that a different, darker tale lies underneath the patina of the obvious. The full story of "The Crimson Weaver" is one that takes some effort to uncover, but ultimately proves rewarding to the diligent reader.

The story starts, after a short preamble that includes an almost mandatory encounter with a gibbering crone, when the Apprentice asks his Master a curious question: "How does passion first touch a man's life?" (9). This sends the Master into a reverie where he recalls a past love, now long lost, and announces:

> Let it suffice that ere I tasted of wedlock the woman died, and her death sealed for ever the door of that chamber of my heart. Yet, if one might see therein, there is an altar crowned with ever-burning tapers and with wreaths of unwithering asphodels. (10)

The asphodel (most likely the white asphodel, *Asphodelus albus*) has long been a symbol of death and of mourning; it was "commonly used to decorate the graves of the departed, from the belief that it afforded nourishment to the manes of the dead" and "was sacred to Proserpine, 'Queen of Shades'" (Lloyd 808). Proserpine, also known as Persephone, is sometimes depicted with the flower entwined in her hair as she gazes out over her melancholy domain. In "Ode on St. Cecilia's Day" (1708), Alexander Pope imagined the scene:

causes her skin to be "deathly white and her lips fretted with pain" (11). Despite what would be an alluringly macabre appearance in any other weird tale, the Master's reaction to her is curious: "My Master still trembled, but he did not move, for the gaze of the woman was fixed upon him. His brows twisted and his white hair rose and stood erect, as if he viewed some unspeakable horror" (11).

After the Crimson Weaver attempts to seduce the Master, foiled only by the Apprentice's frantic admonishment that "the wreaths wither, the tapers bend and fall" (11), the two men flee and find themselves "again on the track we had made in the yew-mast. But twilight was falling [. . .] all was in utter darkness; so at the foot of a tree [. . .] we lay down and slept" (12). The Apprentice suffers strangely delirious dreams of curious times and places—the Castle of the Ebony Dwarf, the Chamber of Gloom, the White Minaret— before waking to find his Master gone, the ashen lock of his lover's hair[1] discarded on the sward. He returns to the palace of the Crimson Weaver, as if through a mist-shrouded dream, where he encounters the surreal "dogs and pigs with human limbs," "a steaming sanguine pool," distorted architecture that sends his own voice back to him in "a babble of echoes" (13), and finally the Crimson Weaver herself, resplendent after having "doffed her tattered robe for one new and lustrous as freshly drawn blood" (13). The narcotic effects of the yew have taken hold.

Here, in this whirl of blood and vapor, is where the horrid denouement of the tale is revealed. The Crimson Weaver reveals the fate of the Master: his body has been rendered down to create yarn for her blood-red robes and then lashes out at the Apprentice with claws "shapen as those of a vulture" (14), the rending talons of the harpy, to draw him into the same fate.

Let us tie these two parts together. The Master dwells upon his memories of a dead lover and the torments that her soul endures whilst condemned to linger in a place of "one long melancholy night." How did she die? "I may not tell you" (9), the Master stutters by way of explanation. Whatever the causes, it rests heavy on him.[2] Then the

---

1. Some commentators believe that the use of σφοδελόν, or "flowery," to describe the meadows of asphodel is incorrect and that it should instead be σποδελόν, "ashy." Is it accidental, then, that the hair of the Master's lover is described as "ash-coloured"?

2. As well as asphodel, Persephone is also associated with the violet. Symbolically, the vio-

pair are consumed by the intoxicating fume of yew-mast and fall into a nightmare realm of "satyrs vomiting senilely, nymphs emptying wine upon the lambent flames of dying phoenixes, creatures that were neither satyrs nor nymphs, nor gryphins, but grotesque adminglings of all, slain by one another, with water gushing from wounds in belly and thigh" (10), formed from the master's guilt and despair. An apparition of his lover returns from the dead, the Master recognizing the "unspeakable horror" of her unnatural appearance. Robed in flesh and granted all the persecutory powers of the harpy,[3] she literally tears his heart to pieces and finally brings him to account.

This identification of the Weaver with the Master's unnamed love adds an interesting and crucial element to the tale. The Weaver is not merely a predatory figure but an avatar of Nemesis, releasing her fury through directed vengeance rather than mere malice. When we realize the origin of her motivation, the redressing of an emotional imbalance, she acts not simply as an antagonist to be overcome or a monster to flee but as a passionate foil to the Master's intellectual rejection of human sympathies. Admittedly, the story is too gauche in this respect to be truly considered a feminist tale, but for the end of the nineteenth century it is progressive at the very least.

What is it that makes "The Crimson Weaver" so exceptional? What makes the abandonment of Gilchrist's body of writing so saddening and yet, like the Master's lover, so ripe for resurrection? It is simply this: his works resonate with a subtle and delicate understanding of how horror so thoroughly infests the world we live in, how it is ever-present in the very sky and soil that surrounds us. It is hard to believe that, with his understanding of nature and Victorian grammar-school education, Gilchrist would be ignorant of the subtleties in the intertwined floral and mythic elements he invokes and how they so often relate to dark truths of existence. The layering and nuance Gilchrist introduces into the narrative cut in many ways to the heart of what horror is about: the lurking shadow, the corruption of our fragile normality, the fear that something we cannot see

---

let represents many things: delicacy and modesty, but also untimely death in the young and resurrection. In John Everett Millais's painting of Shakespeare's Ophelia, she wears violets as she drowns herself.

3. The harpies, the "snatchers," were not simple beasts but wily agents of the vengeful Erinyes, bringing evildoers to account.

is hiding less than a breath away, waiting to snatch us up into the void. For the Master the horror comes from an understanding that his dead lover is not in a place of peace, but of weeping and torment. He recoils from the presence of the Crimson Weaver as much as he needs to feel the oblivion of her embrace.

Gilchrist understands the paradox that all who read horror, who live horror, are wrapped within: the spiralling nausea of needing simultaneously to delve and to retreat. "The Crimson Weaver" is not only a work of horror, it is a work *about* horror; it explores the vertiginous terror of falling into a story so completely that something hidden between the words will grasp us with its vulture claws and not let go, that we shall glance down and see, as the Apprentice sees, "the bloody clew ever unwinding from my heart and passing over the western hills to the Palace of the Siren" (14).

Ultimately, masterfully, Gilchrist decants the three great endings of horror into a rare blend—the Death of the Master, the Insanity of the Apprentice, and the Exile of the Weaver commingling into one another with a sanguine inevitability—and then uses a powerful irony to make this heady draught all the more intoxicating: the more deeply we drink of it, the more deeply we are enthralled.

> And souls of men, who grew beyond their race,
> And made themselves as Gods against the fear
> Of Death and Hell; and thou that hast from men,
> As Queen of Death, that worship which is Fear.
> —Alfred, Lord Tennyson, "Demeter and Persephone"

Works Cited

Bush, Lawrence C. "R. Murray Gilchrist's Short Fiction: A Missing Link between English Decadence and Victorian Feminism." M.A. thesis: California State University, 2010.

Gilchrist, R Murray. "The Crimson Weaver." In *A Night on the Moor and Other Tales of Dread*. [N.p.]: Wordsworth Editions, 2006.

Hageneder, Fred. *Yew*. London: Reaktion Books, 2013.

Homer. *The Odyssey of Homer*. Tr. S. H. Butcher and Andrew Lang. London: Macmillan, 1912.

Lloyd, Mary A. "The Classic Flora." *Galaxy* 18 (July 1874): 115–21.

Lovecraft, H. P. *The Ancient Track: The Complete Poetical Works of H. P. Lovecraft*. Ed. S. T. Joshi. New York: Hippocampus Press, 2013.

Smith, Clark Ashton. *Out of Space and Time*. London: Panther, 1974.

[Unsigned.] "Novel Reviews." *Spectator* (15 March 1902): 23.

The "V" Word
Jose Cruz

T. E. GRAU. *They Don't Come Home Anymore*. [N.p.]: This is Horror, 2016. 104 pp. ISBN: 978-1-910471-03-6. $10.99 tpb.

The word isn't "verboten," although one could say that uttering it either within or without the horror genre is indeed forbidden. The word we refer to, of course, is "vampires." Attaching this deadly phrase to any work of fiction immediately incites a knee-jerk reaction of raised defenses from the audience. Hands snap up to temples and wallets alike to keep migraines at bay and hard-earned cash in check. "Not *them* again," a million people mutter in unison. Much like political candidates and Top 40 songs, vampires have become over-exposed to the point of weariness. Unlike those things, vampires have been around for a lot longer, so by virtue of their street cred they are usually seen as being old, outdated, and all used up.

And yet we still keep coming back to them. For every million people who run shrieking to the hills waving garlic buds and crucifixes, there are a million others clamoring to the bookstores and the cinemas to await the latest hemophagiac epic. That's because for every story that acts as a lazy retread of the myths and halfpenny dramas we've seen a hundred times before, there are still those singular works in every era that manage to surface from the bloody chaff to inject fresh vigor into the desiccated veins of the Undead.

It's very much the same for the artists who create the stories themselves. For all its shopworn tropes, the vampire still possesses totemic power, and the spell it casts can prove too strong to resist. Some respond to this by writing homage. Others attempt to revolutionize the vampire by warping it, beefing it up, or stripping it bare; in short, these writers try to make the vampire *theirs*.

It's clear in reading *They Don't Come Home Anymore,* the new work released from the novella line of This is Horror, that author T. E. Grau has attempted to twist the vampire into different contortions to see what new configuration of terror might come from the endeavor. Grau thankfully wields an exuberant imagination and sincere intentions for the majority of his reinvention, and it is these qualities that keep interest afloat even as the story sadly begins to hobble during the last leg of its journey.

The tale starts out strong and mysterious. Hettie, our protagonist, is grieving with the rest of her community over the sudden onset of leukemia in Avery Valancourt, crown jewel of high school royalty and patron saint of young, white innocence to society at large. Avery is also the subject of Hettie's private obsession. Similar to the character of Alden from Grau's exceptional short story "Tubby's Big Swim," Hettie is a withdrawn misfit who constructs a fantasy relationship with an idealized figure who barely acknowledges her. A fleeting exchange over secreted cigarettes in the school's crumbling restroom is enough to cement Avery as her ultimate BFF in Hettie's mind. With images of Avery's wasting body in the hospital room and thoughts of her imminent fate tainting her every waking moment, Hettie resolves to keep her special friend alive at any cost.

The novella suddenly skips ahead in time, showing Hettie trudging through sewage on broken high heels as a strange kind of death overtakes her. It is a tantalizing and upending development, one decorated with the tactile details of the urban wasteland that served as a special highlight to Grau's debut fiction collection, *The Nameless Dark* (2015):

> Boarded-up store fronts, machine shops, and small factory spaces that once made things that this country couldn't remember, crowded in over the gum-spotted pavement. Faded signs. Corner diners that fueled a different era chased out of the American Dream by torch-bearing misers willing to trade the future of the United States for two dollar socks and ten thousand dollar automobiles. Cheap graffiti that was as bored as it was crude covered everything. All going through the motions of workaday degeneration.

From here the remainder of the story becomes an examination of the events that led Hettie to this sorry state and how she presumably sold her soul in exchange for a terrible immortality. After a day of sneaking into the Valancourts' palatial house and donning articles from Avery's closet in order to solidify their one-sided bond, Hettie drops in on one of her oblivious, excessively liberal parents' "Bad

Movie Nights" wherein her mother and father sit down to watch a "C-grade train wreck" while petting each other like overzealous teenagers. (The fact that Hettie is not invited to join them is only one of a series of telling signs regarding their relationship.) Secretly spying a scene from the vampire film *The Last Boys*—a fictional "knock-off" of Joel Schumacher's 1980s mainstay so close to the original based on Grau's descriptions that one has to wonder why the author simply didn't use the real thing—Hettie becomes smitten and then driven by the idea of supping sacred blood from a holy bottle and thus becoming a wild child of the night.

It is when Hettie begins her search in earnest by performing online research and then visiting occult hobby shops with genuine hope and without a trace of irony that we fully begin to grasp the depth of her psychosis. (That is if the whole "breaking and entering" thing just seemed eccentric at first.) Despite her at-first-glance shocking inability to separate reality from fantasy, Hettie is not someone to be pitied; Grau certainly doesn't depict her as such. As portrayed by the author, Hettie has many more traits that are relatable to the "average" reader than those that might make her appear to be simply a deranged outsider. People placed in turbulent emotional situations, such as those provoked by death or the approach of death, can become tempted to seek out answers and elixirs from even the most ill-reputed and misguided of sources. One need only to switch on certain TV stations to see healers hard at work assuaging the fears of crippled parishioners who come expecting to get their wishes granted with the touch of a hand.

This analogy is clearly linked in the text when Hettie, turned away and disappointed by disastrous encounters with the smarmy owner of a black magic shop and the crass, duplicitous author of a highly popular vampire series, seeks out a more reliable access point into the genuine world of the vampire by means of three coke-snorting, modern-day decadents who in the end only turn out to be members of a bizarre covert cult hunting for new recruits to serve the Lord Jesus Christ. One of the characters who has led Hettie to this subterranean prayer group is attempting to clean up her drug addiction, and though Hettie turns her away as a "Jesus freak" and spurns her for her insane beliefs, she fails to see the deep kinship they actually have. Both are in effect attempting to get their lives together and seeking out the guidance of supernatural beings to pave the way to self-improvement, and all the implicit vampiric imagery associated with Christianity (the drinking of blood from a holy cup, for starters) is missed by the both of them.

Unfortunately, this is right around the time that the novella begins to strain. Grau had shown a slight tendency toward redundancy earlier in the story (e.g., "'Ha-lle-lu-jah!' Ever said with four pronounced syllables like a gospel preacher"), and this trait seems to crop up more frequently as the story progresses. Other elements occasionally take us out of the narrative. Late in the story, Hettie's thoughts are suddenly disrupted when we enter the headspace of a taciturn supporting character for a brief second before returning to our protagonist's viewpoint. During the exchange that ensues between Hettie and the cult member, Hettie whips out a number of sassy comebacks that don't seem to be keeping with the character we've grown accustomed to seeing over the course of her journey. More unexpected than that are revelations that Hettie possesses latent psychic abilities in the form of "the Sight," a kind of super-intuition that makes her especially privy to the world around her. These claims of power have no concrete supporting evidence within the text. If Hettie demonstrated these abilities at all prior to the allusions made in the final chapters, she must have done it on such a covert level that they are hardly worth mentioning after the fact.

These movements seem to precipitate an even more jarring sea-change that comes in the novella's concluding chapter, a twist in the tail that reveals a credulity-straining master plan undertaken by one of the characters and that is delivered in true *a-ha-ha* Hollywood villain fashion. While it can be argued that this revelation and the manner in which it is conveyed *are* in keeping with the character in question, this entire section of the story comes off as just a bit too tidy and superficial. The ideas aren't necessarily bad; they just suffer in the execution. *They Don't Come Home Anymore* shows most keenly in its rough final third that what it is most in need of is another polish and a fiercely critical eye to pick out the small, inconsequential missteps and technical errors in order to stop them from severely accumulating.

Happily, the finer aspects of Grau's novella resonate more deeply and far longer than any detracting material. When that newly contorted iteration of the vampire finally does make its entrance following Hettie's *Waiting for Godot*–esque trials, it is a grand and grotesque entrance, one that seeks to reclaim the image of the vampire from the domain of brooding Gothicism that ensnares it as Hettie witnesses in the early part of her quest. Grau's creature might deny that the dreaded "v" word applies to it, but the origin story that it shares with Hettie as they seal their bargain reveals the creature's history to be a bit more prosaic and traditional than its statements of ageless grandiosity would lead one to believe. Somehow this seems entirely appropriate given all the other characters in the novella. This vampire is no different from them, for all its outward ghastliness; at the end of the day, it's just another lost soul pretending to be a little more special than it really is.

They Don't Come Home Anymore finds a young author stretching his muscles. Though it might pale slightly when placed next to his last successful release, the experience of watching him evolve is still an enjoyable one. This reader looks forward to seeing more new contortions in the future.

Shadows with Teeth

Darrell Schweitzer

ELLEN DATLOW, ed. *The Best Horror of the Year, Volume 8*. New York: Night Shade Books, 2016. 318 pp. ISBN: 978-1-59780-853-8. $15.99 tpb.

It is almost superfluous to review another Ellen Datlow Year's Best anthology. Of course it's good. Datlow has been doing this for a long time. The present volume is part of a successor series, the surviving half of the former *Year's Best Fantasy and Horror* which went on for many years. Datlow always makes the most thorough searches each year; she reads everything, rather than taking the easy way out by grabbing a few obvious names to sell the book and a handful of other writers the editor wishes to favor. The result is that her books will contain surprises, certainly items unfamiliar to most readers. Her summaries are invaluable records of the field, essential reading.

Therefore it is probably useful to attempt some generalizations about the state of the horror field as observable from this book. Yes, of course there are some very strong stories. I'd say that among the standouts are "We Are All Monsters Here" by Kelly Armstrong, which manages to make something new out of both vampire and zombie-apocalypse tropes by combining them, and achieves this through a simple, strong narrative with good characterizations; "Black Dog" by Neil Gaiman, about murder and folk-religion in rural England, a subsequent adventure of Shadow Moon, the protagonist of *American Gods;* and Carmen Marcia Machado's "Descent," which deftly turns very sinister at the end. This story and most of the others follow an aesthetic variously expounded by M. R. James and some others, that at the beginning of the story the supernatural or horrific element may seem an incidental detail, but by the end it has grown in importance until it is central. For example, Reggie Oliver's "The Rooms Are High" is first about an older man vacationing in a seaside resort he hasn't seen since childhood, then about what seems like harmless sexual teasing, then about obsession, predation, and the mysterious description of the "high" rooms in the establishment where he is staying taking on a whole new meaning.

Two of the stories are explicitly Lovecraftian—Lovecraft's images and ideas now being as much part of the mainstream horror idiom as Poe's—but these two, by Steve Rasnic Tem and Tamsyn Muir, are disappointing, as they don't seem to be able to move much beyond the Lovecraftian cliché of the protagonist who exists to reveal the horror, then be eaten. At least Muir's protagonist (in "The Woman in the Hill") accomplishes something or perhaps inspires something to be accomplished. Tem's main character is another old chap on a nostalgic vacation (to the Innsmouth beach front) who more or less dissolves. I think. It's not really clear or very interesting.

Another generalization we can make is that the era of splatterpunks and going for the gross-out is behind us now, and success in modern horror is often a matter of getting the balance between ambiguity and murkiness precisely right. Ambiguity is when the reader knows exactly what is going on but not entirely (or much at all) what it means. Murkiness is a matter of not knowing what is going on. There is a third approach, the Lovecraftian one, in which, in a story like "The Shadow over Innsmouth" or "The Haunter of the Dark," we come to know quite explicitly what is going on *and* what it means, and the horror resonates from the implications. At the other extreme is a story like Robert Aickman's classic "The Hospice," in which a series of disturbing, strange, and seemingly nonsensical events build up to a subtly terrifying climax, and we never find out what is going on or why. The story is like a bad dream. It has all the emotional structure of a conventional horror story without specific plot details, like a tent that mysteriously holds itself up without any poles or stakes and is all that much eerier as a result. John Langan, in "The Underground Economy," not only takes the bold step (for a male writer) of writing from the point of view of female strippers in a "gentlemen's club," but achieves a genuinely Aickmanesque effect. You see what has happened and where the story has gone, but not all the pieces are there. The result is a terrifying mystery. (Not surprisingly, this story was first published in the anthology *Aickman's Heirs*.) The balance is perfect. This is particularly impressive to any fellow practitioner of weird fiction, who knows how hard that is to do.

It has been said of the horror story that it is an inherently conservative form, not politically necessarily, but aesthetically. Perhaps so. Many of these stories hearken back to M. R. James and what he called "characteristics observed to accompany success": contemporary or near-contemporary settings, a strong sense of place (Alaska, rural England, seaside England, New Zealand), and an intrusion of the supernatural into the lives of ordinary people. You don't have to know entirely what kind of predator is out in the woods whimpering "Help me" in Laird Barron's "In a Cavern, In a Canyon," but it is definitely there, and it made off with the protagonist's father long before she once again confronts it. These are all stories about shadows, often shadows with teeth.

Existential and Ontological Horror

S. T. Joshi

JOEL LANE. *This Spectacular Darkness: Critical Essays.* Edited by Mark Valentine and John Howard. Carlton-in-Coverdale, UK: Tartarus Press, 2016. x, 338 pp. ISBN: 978-1-905784-90-5. £35.00 hc.

This book is both long overdue and tragically premature. By that I mean that British author and critic Joel Lane (1963–2013) was planning a full-length treatise on twentieth-century weird fiction, but his sudden and universally lamented death put an end to the plan. Lane had written a number of essays, published in Mark Valentine's *Wormwood,* that would have served as chapters of this treatise; and they, along with Lane's other critical writings, are reprinted here in a book that conclusively demonstrates Lane's keen insight into the essence of weird fiction and his firm grasp of its progression in the last century.

Lane began his critical work surprisingly early. Chronologically, the first essay in this book is "*Strange Eons* and the Cthulhu Mythos," published in 1981, when Lane was eighteen. This strikingly perceptive article may perhaps overvalue Robert Bloch's novel, but it concludes that "The imaginative core created—or discovered—by Lovecraft is a well of ideas that is virtually untapped." Lovecraft devotees may raise their eyebrows at that comment, noting how many Lovecraft-inspired tales were in existence even by 1981; but in fact Lane was quite right. He was well aware that most Cthulhu Mythos stories written up to that time were mechanical imitations of the surface elements in Lovecraft's work rather than elaborations of the "core" of his writing—cosmic alienation, psychic transference, and so on. And even though Lane imprudently (to my mind) praises Brian Lumley in this essay, it nonetheless comes across as a remarkably astute commentary for someone of that age—or any age.

The title essay, previously unpublished, sets the tone for the treatise that Lane was in the process of writing. Here he maintains that weird fiction wasn't really a genre as such prior to the early twentieth century; writers of many different stripes, from Henry James to W. W. Jacobs, dabbled in it from time to time, and it was not cleanly distinguished from mainstream fiction. For a variety of reasons, that changed at the dawn of the last century. Lane goes on to assert that there are two major strands in twentieth-century weird fiction—what he calls "existential horror" and "ontological horror." The latter was what is now generally called "cosmic" or "external" horror, as practiced by William Hope Hodgson, Arthur Machen, H. P. Lovecraft, and others. The former is the intimate, "internal" horror of M. R. James, Ray Bradbury, Richard Matheson, and others.

This is a sound dichotomy and is a useful hermeneutic tool by which to chart the course of weird fiction in the last century. Lane's discussions of Lovecraft can occasionally be a bit simplistic. In addressing that author's lessening output toward the end of his life, Lane writes: "Lovecraft gave up writing fiction because he had ceased to find his own ideas frightening"—a rather crude analysis of a phenomenon that is infinitely complex. But in the essay "World Gone Wrong" Lane studies Lovecraft far more acutely. While properly criticizing some Lovecraft critics for focusing too much on the author's philosophy at the expense of the actual emotive essence of the stories themselves, Lane goes on to discuss key Lovecraft stories from a chronological perspective, showing how the author developed his vision of a "world gone wrong," whether by the incursion of extraterrestrial entities (*At the Mountains of Madness*) or "an alien biological 'taint'" ("The Shadow over Innsmouth"). Lane provocatively states that the ghostwritten story "The Mound" ranks with Wells's *The Time Machine* as "an allegory of the human future." And he also makes an amusing conjecture on the influence of Lovecraft on Dr. Seuss!

A much earlier essay, "The Master of Masks" (1991), studies Lovecraft's invention of the ambiguous entity Nyarlathotep, also tracing its usage in the work of later writers. Lane provocatively claims that the figure of Mr. Dark in Bradbury's *Something Wicked This Way Comes* (1962) is a kind of Nyarlathotep stand-in.

At various points in this book Lane makes a strong case for certain examples of noir crime fiction as genuine contributions to weird fiction, for all their lack of supernaturalism. One of the most penetrating essays in the book is "The Dark Houses of Cornell Woolrich," in which Lane studies the novels and tales of that cheerless author, demonstrating how close his work comes to existential terror. And Lane is surely right, in the essay "The October Country," to champion Ray Bradbury's pioneering of that mode of terror—bringing the weird down from the cosmic spaces to the level of mundane human life. Lane writes of Bradbury's seminal volume, *The October Country* (1955):

> *The October Country* is undoubtedly the most influential postwar book in the weird fiction genre. . . . What it does . . . is to redefine the genre's conditions of possibility: the reasons why horror fiction exists, its thematic roots, its metaphorical agenda. It links the supernatural with human experience in a compelling, and distinctively modern, way. Its impact on later generations of weird fiction writers has been far-reaching and profound.

Lane even makes a brave attempt to defend the merits of some of Bradbury's later work, such as *Death Is a Lonely Business* (1985).

Lane has also written insightful essays on Theodore Sturgeon, Fritz Leiber, and Harlan Ellison—all of whom are, in the opinion of ordinary readers (and perhaps many critics), chiefly science fiction writers, but whom Lane believes to be central figures in weird fiction at mid-century. His essay on Leiber is particularly acute: "Leiber fuses the existential and ontological strands of supernatural horror by connecting their domains: he defamiliarises the human, revealing the unknown in everyday life." I would have liked to see Lane devote more than a single paragraph to the early novel *Conjure Wife* (1943), which to my mind brilliantly updates the weird tale (in this case, the theme of witchcraft) by thrusting it into the contemporary world and by making it more of a psychological than a supernatural phenomenon; but Lane's sensitive analysis of the later novel *Our Lady of Darkness* (1978) makes up for that deficiency.

This Spectacular Darkness contains two essays on Robert Aickman. To me they are not quite as enlightening as they could be, chiefly because for some reason Lane does not discuss the totality of Aickman's weird output. One essay, "Forever Always Ends" (2013), only covers Aickman's writing up to *Sub Rosa* (1968); the other, a much earlier piece entitled "The Double Edge" (1990), does discuss some later works, although such masterful tales as "The Hospice," "Meeting Mr Millar," and "Letters to the Postman" are bypassed.

It is unsurprising that some of the most luminous pages in this book are those devoted to Ramsey Campbell, a Liverpudlian whose excursions into urban horror must have resonated with the Birmingham native whose work is very much in the same mold. There are three separate essays on Campbell in this book (I was privileged enough to have published one of them for the first time in *The Count of Thirty: A Tribute to Ramsey Campbell* [1993] and to have reprinted another in the same book), and each is a masterwork of thematic criticism. To Lane, Campbell is another writer (like Fritz Leiber) who united the existential and ontological threads of weird fiction, and it is unsurprising that Lovecraft, Leiber, and M. R. James are among Campbell's chief influences. Indeed, one of Lane's essays, "Writers in the James Tradition: Ramsey Campbell," is a superb analysis of James's influence on the contemporary writer—and also features some illuminating discussions of the secret of James's own effectiveness as a weird writer.

It is also to be expected that Lane would be sensitive to the appeal of Thomas Ligotti, as that author's bleak view of humanity must also have struck a chord with Lane. And yet, his essay, published in 2010, must have been written before Ligotti published *The Conspiracy against the Human Race* in that same year; otherwise Lane would never have said that Ligotti "does not share the antihumanist perspective of Lovecraft." In fact, Ligotti's treatise establishes that he is a pessimist and misanthrope *par excellence,* subscribing to the contemporary philosophical school of "anti-natalists"—a school that suggests (not without reason, I would say) that human beings would be better off if they had never been born. Nonetheless, Lane writes keenly on the American writer, tracing the influence of Lovecraft, Bradbury, and other writers on him.

This book concludes with four interesting essays about Lane himself. John Howard writes an affectionate but somewhat disjointed memoir that also addresses Lane's work as a literary critic. Mark Valentine supplies an engaging impressionistic account of five early stories by Lane that profoundly affected him, while Mat Joiner writes penetratingly on a little-known body of Lane's work—his several collections of poetry. These are not primarily weird, focusing instead on urban life, left-wing politics, and the complex interplay of love and sex; but Joiner makes a convincing case that they are central to the understanding of Lane's overall oeuvre. And Nina Allen writes with similar perspicacity on Lane's trilogy of novels, *From Blue to Black* (2000), *The Blue Mask* (2003), and *The Missing Tracks* (completed in 2012 but still unpublished). These novels are also not primarily weird; rather, they focus on rock music and the British political scene in the last decade of the twentieth century and the first decade of the twenty-first. They are difficult works, but Allen suggests that they will ultimately prove rewarding to the patient reader.

This single volume establishes Joel Lane as a significant critic of weird fiction. It would have been better if Lane had spent less space in some essays on plot summary and more on analysis of the works in question, but that is a small blemish. Quite literally every page of this book provides some illuminating comment on the author or work being discussed, and the book as a whole can stand as a more than adequate substitute for the cohesive treatise that Lane did not live to write. Every devotee of the weird will find something insightful in this assemblage of critical essays.

In the Heliotherapy Ward

Amber Doll Diaz

Lights Out. Directed by David F. Sandberg; screenplay by Eric Heisserer; produced by James Wan, Lawrence Grey, Eric Heisserer. Cast: Teresa Palmer as Rebecca; Gabriel Bateman as Martin, Rebecca's young brother; Maria Bello as Sophie, Rebecca and Martin's mother; Alexander DiPersia as Bret, Rebecca's boyfriend.

Sometime in the winter of 2013, being a millennial woman of a macabre and impatient fancy, I decided to peruse the annals of YouTube's vast and varied selection of short horror films made by budding cineastes. I imagine these filmmakers serving up refreshing Exorcist-green juices from Whole Foods in a world where cinematic McRib® sandwiches are force-fed to the public, year after year, at the Mall of Hollywood. After a half hour of falling down the rabbit hole of YT's right-hand recommendation sidebar, I came across the selection of uploads by the user ponysmasher. He is better known now as director David F. Sandberg, among the rising band of James Wan aficionados. Sandberg's handful of quality homegrown shorts captured my attention with his effective and cheeky-for-comedic-relief flair. I was intrigued by sprinklings of technology blending with familiar tropes—iPhones in place of the binoculars of *Rear Window* (1954) or the dreadful landlines of *Black Christmas* (1974). The natural acting prowess of his recurring and unconventional leading lady Lotta Losten was both striking and heartening. I became an instant subscriber and devoured his works in the timeliness allotted by this artistic medium. Concluding eventually that his underground popularity was still incubating, I deftly tucked my hipster-knowledge of his creative gifts away in one the back rooms of my memory warehouse.

Fast-forward to winter 2016–17 to find me unsurprised at Sandberg's successful pairing with Eric Heisserer, the screenwriter of *Arrival* (2016), which was itself among the strongest science fiction films of the last decade. What *is* surprising, however, are the rare moments when we horror addicts are wholly refreshed by an original concept amid a barrage of stale like *Paranormal Activity* . . . 6? It behooves me to shed light on the sorrier state we may fall into as a genre if big-name studios did not take risks on short films and independent producers/writers much, much more often. We must never forget that there was once an unknown director who brought his Super 8 camera into the woods in 1978 and shot a 30-minute short film called *Within the Woods*. Of course, Sam Raimi literally had to beg investors for the funding needed for the feature film that would become *The Evil Dead* in 1981.

Luckily, this is not the case with *Lights Out* and its generously stylized production courtesy of New Line Cinema and Warner Brothers' budget of five million dollars. The plot builds on Sandberg's original short, which featured a woman being tormented by a creature whose presence is only revealed when she turns off her hallway light. There is a brief session of uncanny valleyesque fear as she attempts to process what is and isn't right before her eyes. With every flick of the switch, we are led further into the healthy primordial fears we often miss, most of us living in the era of light pollution and constant blue-light exposure. To this backdrop add a dysfunctional family unit plagued by their mother's internal demons, a punk rock Nancy Drew as the rebellious adult daughter who unravels the ghastly history of the monster's origin, and there we have it—an amalgam of vaguely conventional elements that nonetheless strike a new chord in this excellently dramatic film.

The full-length *Lights Out* pairs a classic fear of the dark with the anxieties of the American Generation Y: untraditional family dynamics, the worsening current state of mental health assistance, and a sprinkle of plain stupid jump scares. Even so, horror followers are gifted here, with attentively detailed and near-trademarked James Wan signature set design. In a scene where our female protagonist Rebecca first encounters the heliophobic monster in the middle of night, her room is lit only by a blinking red neon tattoo parlor sign outside her loft window. As the sign flashes on and off, a demonic figure appears and reappears, quickly heightening the tension built slowly and subconsciously through the nightmarish, sanguine tone of the entire room. This crimson wash of light is deeply reminiscent of Wan's use of it in *Dead Silence* (2007), where Billy the Puppet torments another blonde protagonist, bathed completely in a blood-red light from a flashing sign just outside the motel window.

Scenes like this have obviously resonated with my own subconscious, as I was about twelve when *Dead Silence* premiered in theatres, and to my more trained eyes they reveal Sandberg/Wan's astute joint recognition that setting is a character too. The way you dress that character is paramount to the aura and "takeaways" of the film. Sandberg is ever the steward of expositional subtlety, and it is worth praising his judicious decision to give us useful, and economically told, story and character background without wasting screen time on stilted dialogue and unnatural Hermione-esque explanations of information. The viewer enjoys this technique during the opening titles, with a close-up montage of family photos and framed newspaper clippings, framing a story within a story. This was similarly used, to varying degrees of effectiveness, in the *Insidious* and *Saw* franchises, and rarely wears itself this for its versatility. Hopefully, crossover between mainstream production companies and indie filmmakers will become much more commonplace in the future. After all, the first horror film was a three-minute masterwork entitled *Le Manoir du diable* or *The House of the Devil* (1896). (I think we can all agree that Ti West definitely ripped that title off for his own *House of the Devil* [2009].)

Previous critics have deprecated *Lights Out* for the gimmicky nature of the characters' exquisite resourcefulness in finding strategies to combat the darkness, where the film's monster thrives. These assume the form of cellphone lights, car headlights, neon signs, and other contrivances. This plot detail, however, hearkens nostalgically back to the *Nightmare on Elm Street* franchise and, personally, to how much brainstorming and/or nail biting I've done as a too-young kid watching teens come up with increasingly unique ways to stay awake and stay alive. That was always a significant part of these films' fun and suspense. I continue to relish these interactive and imaginative opportunities for deeper immersion in a film's universe. There is usually a need for trial and error in most horror films, which is what lends the viewer a sense of realism and builds on overall tension of dread and doom when our protagonists fail repeatedly to vanquish the evil. Adam breaks his handsaw in trying to escape the bathroom in *Saw* (2004); Laurie Strode attempts to kill Michael by stabbing knitting needles into his neck without success in

Halloween (1978); and Kelly Rowland vainly tries to taunt Freddy Kruger to death in *Freddy vs. Jason* (2003). The characters we imprint ourselves upon needed to get creative to live, and we are all the more creative in reality for it.

That said, I also can't in good conscience sign off on what is easily one of the most problematic film endings I've seen presented in recent memory. What *Lights Out* does well practically ruptures entirely under the mass of what it has royally botched. In 2016 it was announced that New Line Cinema and Warner Brothers Pictures have greenlit a sequel, which I find to be a wise decision due to the following: *Lights Out* insensitively uses the plot point of the character Sophie's suicide—an act of self-sacrifice to save her children—as a neat way of wrapping up this film. Oxymoronic as it seems, *Lights Out* was lazily rushed to a totally unsatisfying and frankly irresponsible conclusion. This kind of thoughtless writing simply cannot be allowed to exist in the absence of a spotlight and further discussion. Perhaps I expected too much from a film working around a fictional monster with the simplest Achilles' heel, but I know these particular production teams can do better. For most families living with the mentally ill, the suicide of any member has likely never been a feasible coping option. The only redeemable option for New Line Cinema and Warner Brothers Pictures (among the other four production companies in assistance) would be to address and correct this issue in the upcoming sequel. The pending plotline must make abundantly clear to the audience that suicide generally resolves nothing, and only that will have made good what is in my opinion an egregious ethical error.

Ultimately, *Lights Out* is a well-conceived, if haphazardly finalized, film about the murkiest bogs of untreated mental illness, which have plagued American families on a larger scale than even the diluted horror cinema we defeatedly consume again and again in recent years. Even so, I feel certain we're approaching a state in which aspiring filmmakers may dare, in an age of incessant remakes and sequels, to create and dream. I like to think of their overhead lightbulbs resolutely blazing in the darkness.

The Horror in the Card Catalog

S. T. Joshi

DARRELL SCHWEITZER and JOHN ASHMEAD, ed. *Tales from the Miskatonic University Library*. Hornsea, UK: PS Publishing, 2017. xv, 201 pp. ISBN: 978-1-78636-028-1: £40 (signed/limited hc). ISBN: 978-1-786360-29-8: £20 (trade hc).

The "forbidden book" is a well-worn theme in H. P. Lovecraft's work, and it can be found in his earliest as well as his latest tales. The Pnakotic Manuscripts were cited so early as "Polaris" (1918), while the genesis of his most celebrated imaginary tome, the *Necronomicon,* can be traced to the passing mention of Abdul Alhazred and his "unexplainable couplet" in "The Nameless City" (1921), and then to the citation of the actual volume in "The Hound" (1922). The idea is a complex and variegated one in Lovecraft, perhaps suggesting this lifelong bookworm's pensive hope that the secrets of the universe were to be dug out of rare and obscure books if one could only find them. These books contain such dreadful truths about our own tenuous place in the universe that we explore them only at our peril.

But even in Lovecraft's day—and especially as his literary colleagues began adding their own fanciful titles to the ever-growing library of arcane treatises—the notion became something of a shtick. Lovecraft himself made the aging Henry Armitage, the librarian at Miskatonic University, an implausible hero in "The Dunwich Horror" (1928), defeating the Whateley clan's plans to let in the Old Ones; but thereafter, the whole "forbidden book" motif began to lose its power through sheer overuse. When, in the late story "The Haunter of the Dark" (1935), we encounter such a passage as this—"He had himself read many of them—a Latin version of the abhorred 'Necronomicon', the sinister 'Liber Ivonis', the infamous 'Cultes des Goules' of Comte d'Erlette, the 'Unaussprechlichen Kulten' of von Junzt, and old Ludvig Prinn's hellish 'De Vermis Mysteriis'"—we simply gloss over the farrago of citations and wait impatiently for the actual story to gain momentum.

In the first several decades after Lovecraft's death, the Cthulhu Mythos increasingly became a source of derision—in large part because its devotees, most notably August Derleth, seemed to believe it was sufficient to "add" a tale to the Mythos merely by inventing some new book or god or town (usually in New England, or maybe in the Southwest or even in England). This is why readers were afflicted with such ludicrous abominations as *Cthaat Aquadingen* or *The Ponape Scriptures.*

And yet, as Lovecraft scholarship advanced and showed that the Mythos (and Lovecraft's work in general) really wasn't just about imaginary tomes or outlandish gods, but was instead an expression of a bleak, unflinching comprehension of the insignificance of humanity and of all earth life, some writers chose to use the "forbidden book" topos in a more serious way. Thomas Ligotti's "Vasterien" seems on the surface to be nothing but a hackneyed expression of a standard Lovecraftian motif—a man finds a book and it drives him mad—but what a wealth of dense imagery and intellectual substance lies behind this simple notion! For the book in question seems to embody "the summit or abyss of the unreal, that paradise of exhaustion, confusion, and debris where reality ends and where one may dwell among its ruins." Fred Chappell's "The Adder" presents the terrifying image of the original Arabic version of the *Necronomicon*, titled *Al Azif,* wiping out the texts of other books with which it comes into contact—a potent symbol of the intellectual nihilism of "forbidden" knowledge.

Which brings us at last to *Tales from the Miskatonic Library.* This slim original anthology seeks to reinvest the "forbidden book" motif with new terror and imaginative vigor, but it does so with only middling success. At least one of the editors brings impressive credentials to the task. Darrell Schweitzer has edited a number of successful Lovecraftian anthologies, including *Cthulhu's Reign* (2010) and *That Is Not Dead* (2015). And given that PS Publishing recently issued its own exquisite hoax book catalog, Nate Pedersen's *The Starry Wisdom Library* (2014), it was the logical publisher for this book.

The thirteen stories in this book range widely in tone, impact, and quality. Some authors simply resign themselves to the inevitable and write openly comic or parodic stories, not entirely without success. Marilyn "Mattie" Braden's "The Way to a Man's Heart" tells of a wife, frustrated by a lack of attention (especially between the sheets) from her husband, a professor at Miskatonic, finds a copy of the *Gastronomicon* and whips up a shoggoth soufflé—with predictable, or perhaps not so predictable, results. Alex Shvartsman's "Recall Notice" is a short epistolary tale in which the librarian Blaine Armitage demands that H. W. P. Lovecraft III (great-great-grandson of Lovecraft—a neat trick, since Lovecraft had no offspring) return the books he has checked out from the library. Instead, a world cataclysm ensues, and at the end we find that one Ian Whateley has replaced Armitage as librarian.

Few stories, indeed, are able to escape an undercurrent—intentional or otherwise—of the comic, even when telling of apocalyptic horrors engulfing the world. Don Webb's "Slowly Ticking Time Bomb" has all manner of in-jokes—on the first page we learn of an event called "MoundCon in Binger, Oklahoma," a reference to Lovecraft's ghostwritten novella "The Mound"—but otherwise it tells the tale of a book dealer who reads something called the *Ool Athog Chronicles,* tries one of its spells, and manages to cure his mother of cancer. Far more baleful results soon follow, but the story cannot quite escape a suspicion of deadpan self-parody.

Rather more successful is Adrian Cole's "The Third Movement," which appears to be set in the New York of several decades ago, as it narrates a story alternating between supernatural horror and hard-boiled crime fiction. Here the tome in question is the *Malleus Tenebrarum* (Hammer of Darkness), which a mysterious figure named Vermilion is seeking. The tale becomes increasingly grim and foreboding as it takes us into an unknown underground cavern where the book and its "guardian" are found. A. C. Wise's "The Paradox Collection" fuses terror and pathos in its account of a slim pamphlet titled *Sexing the Weird,* by one C. S. Bryant—who proves to be a woman whose ghost a young librarian at Miskatonic encounters in the library. Douglas Wynne's "The White Door" is a brief and chilling story of a book, *The White Death,* that "reveals a true account of the realms beyond death." But the trick is that it tells a different story to every reader: can it be that the book reveals the manner of each person's death?

One of the best stories in the book is P. D. Cacek's "One Small Change." Here a middle-aged librarian, Eleanor McCormack, afflicted both with a stutter and with a young boss, Taylor Dickson, who habitually torments her, finds herself having to deal with an interlibrary loan request by a professor, R. E. Bennett. He wants to take the book out of the library, but the book—which had come from

Miskatonic—is not permitted to leave the building. McCormack herself takes the book home—and interesting results follow.

Schweitzer's own tale, "Not in the Card Catalog," features a work called *The Book of Undying Hands*. Not only is the book "older than time, older than mankind on this planet," but it is *still being written*—and every new "contributor" to the book finds his or her essence absorbed into the book, with their hands holding its covers closed. This grisly premise is the trigger for an action-packed tale whose numerous twists and turns leave the reader breathless. Not as successful is James Van Pelt's "The Children's Collection," where a man hired to run the children's collection at the Kingsport Public Library learns of a secret "children's special collections" room stocked with books by local authors, and accessible only by the older residents of the town. The story resolves itself a bit too quickly—further development would have been beneficial.

Some authors resort to the tried-and-true *Necronomicon* as the springboard for their tales. Harry Turtledove, who seems of late to have gained a taste for Lovecraftian fiction (he contributed a piquant story to my *Madness of Cthulhu* anthology), tells of a sinister Arab who wants to borrow the *Necronomicon* and take it back to a professor in Egypt (who in fact is allied with the Islamic State). At the end of the story we learn that reading a spell from the book not unexpectedly leads to disaster ("slime and tentacles and darkness overwhelmed them"). Will Murray's novelette "A Trillion Young" focuses on Olaus Wormius's Latin translation of the *Necronomicon*, even though he (perhaps deliberately) refers to Olaus's Danish name as Ole Worm (actually Ole Wurm). Let it also pass that Murray presents yet another faulty translation of the word *Necronomicon*—"The Laws of the Book of the Dead," a variant of the equally erroneous "Book of the Laws of the Dead." It is tiresome that so many people without the slightest knowledge of Greek etymology have so confidently propounded ridiculous translation of this term, which simply means "Book about the Dead" (or possibly "Book Classifying the Dead"). In any case, in this story world cataclysm also results, although the emphasis is on both biological and computer viruses.

But the best story in the book, unexpectedly, is "To Be in Ulthar on a Summer Afternoon," by the Tasmanian writer Dirk Flinthart. It is extremely difficult to write a successful story set in Lovecraft's Dreamlands, but Flinthart has turned the trick in his account of a book called *The Dream Journal of Arpan the Elder*. The narrator, a man named Bill Drake, has ventured to Ulthar because the book is overdue from the Miskatonic University Library! This is only the beginning of a narrative that melds the perfumed delicacy of Dunsanian fantasy with an underlying grimness that is only manifested in the tale's cheerless conclusion.

Robert M. Price's "The Bonfire of the Vanities" seeks to wipe all its predecessors out by postulating that the entire Special Collections department of Miskatonic has been destroyed by a fire, evidently set by a Christian fundamentalist. This causes the elderly librarian Ezra Pepperidge to engage upon a long quest to restore the choicest titles from the collection, including the *Book of Eibon,* von Junzt's *Nameless Cults,* Prinn's *Mysteries of the Worm,* and of course the *Necronomicon*. How Pepperidge sets about his arduous task, and what its upshot proves to be, must not be told here.

I would not say that there are any transcendentally brilliant tales—analogous to the Ligotti and Chappell stories I cited earlier—in this book, but it is an enjoyable and occasionally powerful anthology that shows that some mileage is still left in the "forbidden book" motif, as in Lovecraftian fiction generally.

I am forced to remark that the copyediting of this book leaves a great deal to be desired. Ordinarily I would not comment on poor or nonexistent copyediting, because these features are (especially in the small press) now the norm rather than the exception. But here the shoddiness exceeds all bounds of tolerance. Why does one writer spell the name of a celebrated character in "The Dunwich Horror" as "Lavinia Whatley," but another (correctly) as "Lavinia Whateley"? How does Will Murray get away omitting the diaeresis (umlaut) on the well-known exclamation "Iä!"? In Cacek's story, the central character is named Bennet early in the text but Bennett later on. Don Webb's story is nearly unintelligible, with a plethora of ridiculous grammatical and stylistic errors, including that erstwhile bane of the grammarian, "it's" for "its." And so on and so forth, ad infinitum, ad nauseam. What will it take for presses large and small to hire capable copyeditors and proofreaders? More terrifying still, are there any such persons left in the world?

Southern Discomfort and the Ubiquitous Undead

Stephanie Graves

ERIC GARY ANDERSON, TAYLOR HAGOOD, and DANIEL CROSS TURNER, ed. *Undead Souths: The Gothic and Beyond in Southern Literature and Culture*. Baton Rouge: Louisiana State University Press, 2015. 308 pp. ISBN: 978-0-8071-6107-4. $42.50 hc.

"*How* and *why* is the South so undead?" This is the central question driving this anthology, and in its twenty essays the authors provide both complex and nuanced answers. Rather than merely retreading the familiar territory of the Southern Gothic, Anderson et al. have assembled a collection that acknowledges this tradition but also seeks to complicate any reductive readings, including "noncanonical" texts that foreground the contemporary immediacy of the Southern dead, thus positing an "undead" influence even in the absence of supernatural occurrence. Many of the essays move away from the traditional Southern Gothic tropes and instead investigate the pluralistic figurations of the undead in Southern culture, considering the undead as "an unruly means of political and social confrontation." By considering diverse perspectives and readings of undeadness, *Undead Souths* tackles issues of race, ethnicity, and economics alongside political and historical anxieties informed by the pervasive image of the undead.

This broad approach to the phenomenon of the Southern undead includes essays informed by Caribbean and postcolonial theory, Native American studies, critical race theory, and even trauma studies. The volume includes considerations of Gothic stalwarts such as Poe and Faulkner, yet considers these texts in new ways. Eric Gray Anderson's essay "The Fall of the House of Po' Sandy: Poe, Chesnutt, and Southern Undeadness" looks at the "haunted voices and spaces" in Poe's "The Fall of the House of Usher" and Charles Chesnutt's "Po' Sandy" as parallel epicenters of undeadness. Essays by Melanie Benson Taylor and Elizabeth Rodriguez Fielder both address the metaphor of the undead and the obsessive relationship to the past in Faulkner; more unexpectedly, Sacha Morrell links the exploitative labor practices and racial oppression of the nineteenth century with the fiction of Herman Melville, particularly in his 1849 satire *Mardi*. Essays by Kirstin L. Squint, Annette Trefzer, and Rain Prud'homme C. Gomez are welcome pieces that consider the undead in Indigenous voices; Squint and Trefzer both address Choctaw culture in the fiction of LeAnne Howe and the importance of the healing presence of the Native undead, while Gomez considers the "carefully crafted southern tapestry" of regionalism in Jeremy Love's webcomic *Bayou* from the perspective of Indigenous Gulf peoples. Although not "undead" in a traditional sense, for Gomez, the trauma of displacement is, through its usual elision in Southern literature, a trauma that is constantly reinscribed; Love's work acknowledges this multitude of Indigenous cultures and "allows a space for trauma to be present, not historic." The inclusion of these Native American voices not only addresses significant gaps in critical conceptions of Southern identity, but it further expands what the editors consider "undead" in relation to the South.

To the volume's benefit, it considers multimodal discourse regarding sites of undeadness. In the standout "What Remains Where: Civil War Poetry and Photography Across 150 Years" by Elizabeth Bradford Frye and Coleman Hutchison, the authors consider the lingering echoes across time between primary poetry and photography of the Civil War-era South and modern works concerned with the indelible nature thereof, foregrounding the refusal of the cultural past to stay buried. Amy Cluskey considers the Haitian postbellum plantation as a site of horror in the 1932 film *White Zombie,* while Leigh Anne Duck focuses on the repetition of undead elements in filmic representations of Southern mountain culture in films such as *Deliverance, The True Meaning of Pictures,* and *Winter's Bone*. Taylor Hagood's essay "Going to Ground: The Undead in Contemporary Southern Popular Culture Media and Writing" seeks to contextualize the current proliferation of the Southern undead evident in popular fiction, graphic novels, and television, focusing on Charlaine Harris's Sookie Stackhouse series of novels and the adapted HBO series *True Blood,* AMC's *The Walking Dead* and Robert Kirkman's graphic novel source text, and the comic book series *The Goon* by Eric Powell. Hagood investigates this "textual cluster" of the undead creature in contemporary media as a tool for both inscribing and combating anxieties regarding authenticity that infuse work which relies on a Southern setting.

Although it may at first glance seem a peculiar editorial choice that the text is not separated into thematic sections or arranged by some grand taxonomy, the essays in the volume are nonetheless closely linked, and they inform one another in such a way that this arrangement becomes less peculiar as each piece is considered in turn. Stylistically, one complaint is that rather than a bibliography for each essay, there is a single comprehensive works cited list that makes cross-researching the references in a particular essay somewhat more cumbersome. However, the index is both comprehensive and thorough, and serves as a great tool for readers. *Undead Souths* may frustrate readers seeking critical work about the literal shambling dead, but the use of the undead as metaphor and mode offers a more comprehensive view of horror in works relating to the region. As scholar Susan V. Donaldson offers in her afterword, the essays in this text "resist and dismantle inherited master narratives" about the South, and indeed, they point toward the transnational global fabric of what we typically consider the South. The diverse criticism in *Undead Souths* would be a benefit to the shelf of anyone interested in complex constructions of the tension between the animate and inanimate in the necrologically obsessed South.

Forever I'm Alone with You

Jose Cruz

LYNDA E. RUCKER. *You'll Know When You Get There*. Dublin: Swan River Press, 2016. 174 pp. ISBN: 978-1-78380-013-1. €30.00 hc.

Horror has always been a genre of great displacement and disturbance. In terms of its more popular examples, this has normally taken shape in narratives that deal with invasions from outside forces, tangible threats that have come to prey upon physical and spiritual flesh and to taint the once-calm waters of complacent reality like Lovecraft's horrible Colour throbbing like a sour heart at the bottom of Nahum Gardner's well.

In less-traveled byways of horror fiction we see a different strain of displacement, one that finds the alien force to be within ourselves.

Through the sensations of the protagonists, we come to realize that *we* are the Colours at the bottom of the well, constantly out of step with the familiar landscape around us, offsetting in our foreignness, hungering for contact and yet destroying anyone that dares come within orbit of our poisonous touch. Many of the characters in Lynda E. Rucker's latest collection, *You'll Know When You Get There,* face similar predicaments: human driftwood caught in the tug of opposing tides, torn between going back to the place they came from, staying in the place they are now, moving toward the place they should be, and restlessly hunting for the place they always dreamed. Sometimes there is one location that represents all these things. Frequently, where the characters eventually end up is in a place that they could never conceive, for better and worse.

This comparatively slim collection—nine tales in all and Rucker's second following *The Moon Will Look Strange* from Karoshi Books—settles gently onto readers' shoulders like the hand of an old friend before yanking them by the collar. "The Receiver of Tales" utilizes a clear and powerful central image: that of the "stories" one carries being literally carved into the flesh, an idea that harkens back to Clive Barker's *Books of Blood* and Ray Bradbury's *The Illustrated Man.* The story is a bit too ephemeral to register a real impact, but it introduces us to themes and characters that will crop up time and again throughout Rucker's works, namely that of a woman choosing to live in relative isolation within "a palace of ink," as apt a metaphor for a personal library as much as a tenement scrawled floor to ceiling with words. She, like so many of Rucker's leading players, is someone who prefers to relate to stories about people rather than the people themselves.

"Widdershins" is more concrete in intent, this time taking the perspective of an American man who retreats to the frigid Irish midlands following a divorce, this being one of a variety of failed relationships in the book. Chronicling his search for a spring on the property surrounding "the old Kelly place" in a diary he takes up on a whim, the man finds that his lonely wanderings have brought him into the company of a strange, foxlike familiar that just might be a sign that things have only started to go "against the sun" for him, if not the entire world. "Widdershins" has Rucker working in pure ghost story form, and it makes for a pleasing terror if ever there was one. Even at this early point in the collection we start to get a true sense of the author's assured talent, her enviable ease of making the acts of both reading and writing feel and look so wonderfully easy. The genuine chills, needless to say, come just as gracefully.

"The House on Cobb Street" finds Rucker firing on all cylinders, tearing the haunted manse of the Gothic age up by the roots and planting it within the neatly quartered lots of Southern middle-class suburbia, imbuing her "bad place" with a convincingly malign mentality pitted against an unwitting married couple. This is another story that uses the epistolary format to its distinct advantage, compiling blog posts and book excerpts along with third-person insights into the wife's tortured psyche in an attempt to compile a full picture of the mysterious tragedy at the story's heart, but which only succeeds in highlighting that which remains enticingly absent from it.

Though not made to be the express focal point of the story, relationships play another subdued but significant key in the narrative's horror. After her husband commits a terrible act, his wife becomes convinced that the house influenced him to do it. And though there is certainly enough evidence to prove her theory correct, her instant refutation is interesting in that it absolves her husband of any premeditated thought and places the blame solidly on a supernatural interloper. The possibility that the wife just might not have fully realized the type of person her husband was appears incomprehensible to her. For her, it is far easier to admit the existence of a haunted house than to consider the idea that she never truly knew the man she loved. And the funny thing is that this reviewer believes it is safe to say that many of us, if placed in her position, would feel the same.

While other protagonists in the collection end up rejecting the settings they feel trapped within or drifting listlessly through, "The House on Cobb Street" offers a haunting role reversal in which the setting rejects its inhabitants, expressly seeking to expunge them from its body like tumors and destroying every remaining bit of their cancerous existence. Rucker likens the ordeal faced by the wife and her house to living in an abusive relationship, and the parallels run disturbingly deep. After permanently "ending" the relationship, we are led to believe that the house goes on a conscious mission to clear up all signs of its "guilt," erasing memories of the married couple and promoting doubt that they ever existed at all. This development works just fine in the context of creating an atmosphere of weird and ominous portent for the purposes of a horror tale, but it also serves as an unsettling reminder of just how short our memories really are and how silenced victims generally remain that way forever. Who needs a haunted house to do all the grunt work when we've already proven to be so good at forgetting about people?

The oldest story in the collection, "Where the Summer Dwells," proves that Rucker had begun to come fully into her own as early as half a decade ago. It deals with nostalgic reminiscences with none of the cloying sweetness that can be frequently packaged with the exercise. Rucker, a native of the American South who now resides in Europe, seems to be saying goodbye to her home here, acknowledging her past while simultaneously parting ways with it in the way she knows best. The nostalgia that is stirred up by the dull heat of a Georgia summer, a set of disused railroad tracks leading to fantastic lands of demon hounds and magical pacts, and the comfortable company of old, dependable, imperfect friends are offset by the grim reminder that nags the mind of any person who has ever tried to recapture a bit of his or her youth's elusive fairy dust: there is no going back, no matter how hard you wish for it.

At this point *You'll Know When You Get There* becomes an excursion in ratcheting expectations: just when readers think they have a handle on Rucker or that the next story couldn't possibly be as good as the last, the author shifts her game plan, explores pet motifs from a new angle and with refreshed energy, incorporates revisionist readings of classic texts, and any number of other wonderful, surprising ploys.

"Who Is This Who Is Coming?" is a postmodern examination of the Jamesian tale that could easily rival any of that old provost's disquieting yarns. Fern Blackwell, another in a line of Rucker's recluses, takes the opportunity to use her vacation time to undertake a walking tour of the English countryside, specifically all the notable locations that were used in the filming of episodes from the old *Ghost Story for Christmas* specials. Small inconveniences rack up to leave her trip with a less-than-desirable pallor, particularly the well-meaning interruptions and commandeering of a fellow "antiquarian" whom Fern meets one night at the inn's pub where she's staying. (Yet again, even after finding someone that she feels she can finally relate to, Rucker's protagonist ends up cloistering herself away.) In this way, as well as in her decision to forego human companionship and invite the otherworldly into her life, Fern is similar to lead characters who have come before her. Here the supernatural takes the shape of a ghostly stalker that may or may not be following her, and for Fern this distant figure represents a chance to escape her drab existence and to live a moment from one of her treasured television dramas, no matter how horrible it might be. Once again, Rucker manages to unstring a few nerves during the climax when she deigns to allow Fern's wish to be granted.

"The Queen of the Yellow Wallpaper" involves another house with more rooms than it lets on. A husband and wife trek out to the desolate, once-grand familial estate of the husband's playwright sister; that the estate is named "Carcosa" will not escape certain readers in the audience. The playwright has been suffering from a psychological relapse into old neuroses that happens to coincide with the composition of her newest production, a play that tells of the arrival of an unseen but oft-alluded-to queen. Meanwhile, our wandering wife has begun to note subtle changes in the house's makeup, particularly in the second-story turret where the sickly-yellow wallpaper lurks. The links to Robert W. Chambers's fiction are more overt than those to the landmark story by Charlotte Perkins Gilman, yet Rucker stylishly weaves in themes of patriarchal suppression and pulsing madness carried over from the Gilman for this amalgamation. Take the wife's early misgivings regarding her husband's good intentions and the pecking order of marriage in general:

> It came upon us gradually, as these things do, this intertwining; there were the career goals that clashed, practically and geographically; late nights and tears, a counsellor to talk us through it all because we are responsible middle-class people who don't give up on a marriage without a fight, and in the end a capitulation on my part. Did I say capitulation? I mean compromise, of course.

While sisterhood was represented in Gilman's story as a shadow-sorority of creeping women lurking beneath wallpaper, Rucker ups the ante and indulges in the baroque imaginings of Chambers's King in Yellow mythos by uniting her two female players in a front against oh-so-assured male reasoning (or "mansplaining," as the kids say) and introducing the reckoning of an almighty queen who reveals our coldly logical husband for the lost, naked babe in the woods that he is.

"The Wife's Lament" is perhaps the collection's most beguiling work. A bizarre modern-day parable, it follows the whirlwind romance and marriage of Penny and Ian, a young American woman and a British man several years her senior whose obscure professional life forces him to make frequent travels. That Penny knows little of what her new husband does for a living stems partly from Ian's overall reticence but mainly from the fact that Penny has been too caught up in the rush of impulsivity to find out much of anything about him. Though they are married and at first passionately in love, Penny's move to Ian's lonely English flat reveals the truth to her: for all intents and purposes, she and her husband remain virtual strangers to each other. This being a Rucker story, one can't help but doubt that this discord would have changed at all given time.

The motives of the couple's chipper neighbor and Ian's longtime friend Fiona act as further fuel to the fiery doubt beginning to eat away at Penny's insides. It all starts coming to a head when Penny encounters a feral woman in a nearby wood who leaves behind a brooch that has ties to an Old English lyric, one that tells of a wife's fall from grace into a seething grave of paranoia and self-fulfilling prophecy. Rucker controls her plot with expert and exquisite skill, carefully managing it with the clockwork precision of a tense psychological thriller while simultaneously generating an aura of nightmarish chaos. It's a heady mix that leaves the reader as gloriously distrustful and discombobulated as the heroine.

"This Time of Day, This Time of Year" turns the mood down a few notches from the manic to the elegiac as a teenage girl attempts to process the inexplicable return of her military sister from a death-drenched tour in the Middle East. The older sister seems to be suffering from an intense form of shellshock, despondent and obtaining only minimal nourishment until she and her younger sibling head out to the ramshackle lakeside cabin of their uncle, another scarred veteran of war.

As in previous entries, this story spotlights secret histories that are gradually discovered by the protagonists, here in the form of another ominously named locale, Hekate, an early-century town that was abandoned and then flooded by the waters that now compose Sorrow Lake. The story's fantastic elements actually pale in comparison to the stark horror of the elder sister's time spent in Afghanistan, which she can only speak of in spare, cryptic phrases. Just when it looks as if the narrative is offering another study of two people in a relationship who are stuck on different planes of existence, the story's conclusion is buoyed with the rediscovery of familial roots and the renewal of purpose.

Closing out the collection is the hypnotic "The Haunting House," the second story original to the book, along with "Who Is This Who Is Coming?" From its very inception, Rucker lulls us into a feeling of somnambulistic calm that she gradually twists into deeper, darker levels of sleep with each recitation of the poetic opening lines:

> This. This house. This door, that sticks on opening. This worn old red stair runner, and the softness of a banister smoothed by generations of hands. This old clock on the landing, this little window, this turn in the stairs as they double back on themselves. This, the second storey, the narrow hallways and the friendly heavy cream-coloured doors with cosy rooms on the other side of them.

This is the persistent dream of Lucy, a young woman renting someone else's room in a shared house with a handful of other boarders, a far cry from the beautiful real estate that her mind calls up every night during sleep. Lucy would be considered, in the parlance of the times, a screw-up. Nurtured in wealth and opportunity, she has not fought or truly worked for anything she's wanted a day in her life, and now, aside from the occasional random act of Yuletide charity, she can barely summon the energy to act like anything but a ghost to her own life. There is only one insane hope she clings to: one day, she will find the haunting house of her dreams.

Lucy, whose identity feels so transient that she frequently thinks her name is "Shawna," the original owner of her room, is perhaps the ultimate Rucker protagonist, Lovecraft's dreadful Colour given shape in the body of a disaffected slattern who seems to have surveyed the wreckage of all the other failed and disillusioned relationships in this collection and decided that human companionship simply isn't worth the effort. This thinking seems to reflect a certain mindset of the artist: why engage with the real world and all its inevitable disappointments when there is perfection waiting for you in the pages of a book, or the safety of a dream?

For someone who has nothing but burned bridges left behind her, it is ironic that Lucy should find her ultimate deliverance within the crumbling walls of a ruined house. But in the end, for better or worse, she has found a new place to call home, much as the British spellings in this story attest to Rucker's own migration to the place where she feels that she belongs.

And that is, of course, what all characters in horror fiction, be they ghost or girl, are struggling to find: a place to call one's own, even if they must live in it on their own. With any luck Rucker's collection will find itself a home on the shelves of countless readers who revel at the sight of masters of the craft at work.

For within this palace of ink they will find a most haunting companion.

Stranger Things: A Conversation between Bev Vincent and Hank Wagner

Author Bev Vincent and critic Hank Wagner discuss the surprising Netflix original drama *Stranger Things*.

HW: So Bev, regarding *Stranger Things,* I perceive several schools of thought out there. Those who absolutely loved it, those who loved it with some reservations, and those that didn't seem to care for it, primarily because they personally felt it was too derivative. Personally, I fell into the first camp. I enjoyed the storytelling and spotting the myriad 1980s-derived Easter eggs with which the Duffer Brothers seeded the narrative.

BV: I washerriff. s intrigued with the show when I saw the first trailer, and decided to watch it based on very little information. I binge-watched it over a two-day period. Two episodes one Friday night and six the following day. I, too, enjoyed noticing the references and the homages. I found myself tweeting things like: "It's Stand by Me meets ET meets Firestarter meets Altered States meets . . ." I'm not a child of the '80s—I lived through them, of course, but my childhood was mostly in the '70s. And yet I enjoyed spotting all the '80s props, from the Realistic-brand walkie talkie to the *Dungeons & Dragons* game.

HW: I caught some of the initial buzz via Facebook and sought the show out on Netflix. I was hooked for the duration (eight hours) within a few minutes.

So let me summarize the story, to frame things. Set in 1983, in the quiet town of Hawkins, Indiana, *Stranger Things* follows the adventures of four young boys as they encounter a creature from a parallel reality. One of their number is actually captured by that creature; the show depicts their reactions to that, and the reactions of the adults around them, primarily focusing on the missing boy's mother and brother, and the town's sheriff. The boys also come into contact with the mysterious U.S. Department of Energy/Hawkins Laboratory, a shadowy government research organization responsible for opening a pathway to our world for the creature, and one of its test subjects, a female escapee goes by the name of Eleven.

BV: The story involves three different generations. First, there are the young kids, the four boys and, later, Eleven. They will certainly remind viewers of the boys from *Stand by Me/The Body* and the Losers from *It*. They're geeky and funny and totally kids, but they're also smart and resourceful. They stay in touch by walkie talkie. When they're confronted with problems, they figure out how to solve them (sometimes with the help of a supportive science teacher). They're true friends. Then there are the older kids, the teenagers. One is the missing boy's brother, another is his best friend's sister. They remind me of the teens from *Carrie,* with all the meanness and casual cruelty. Then there are the adults—the missing boy's mother and the sheriff, both of whom have complicated and compelling backstories of their own. There are many more characters than these, but this is the core group that we get to know over the course of eight hours.

HW: The kids will also make you think of the gang in Spielberg's *The Goonies*. Spielberg's influence is all over this thing, from the aforementioned *ET* to *Close Encounters of the Third Kind*. I thought of him every time someone used a flashlight.

The older teens were an interesting lot. Stock characters/archetypes for the most part, but not stock fates. For instance, the sexually active kids were not harmed or killed by the evil creature, as they surely would have been in any '80s movie. In fact, the person who suffered the most was the ultimate "good girl," a character named Barbara "Barb" Holland, best friend of one of the chief teen leads, Nancy Wheeler. We eventually learn that Barb met a truly horrific end, but she didn't "deserve" it in any way. Her fate in the series triggered many an Internet conversation as to how women are handled on television these days.

That said, let's talk about the three female leads in the series, Nancy Wheeler (Natalia Dyer), Joyce Byers (Winona Ryder), and Eleven, a.k.a. Jane Ives (Millie Bobby Brown).

BV: I first saw Millie Bobby Brown in *Intruders,* the 2014 BBC series based on Michael Marshall Smith's novel of the same name. She played a little girl who had to channel an old man, and she was incredible in it. She had all the mannerisms of an elderly, foul-mouthed guy down pat. Then she was in an episode of *Grey's Anatomy* and at first seemed to be an innocent little girl—but based on *Intruders* I had a bad feeling, and I was right! She has an amazing talent. She has very little dialogue, so she has to act and re-act, to be present when the other characters are talking. Winona Ryder is a little more polarizing. We first meet her character in distress—we don't get to see her under normal circumstances—so she can be a little hard to take at times. But even her character realizes how crazy some of her claims must seem to others. The audience knows she isn't crazy, but no one else does, and even she can't be sure. I liked her scenes with Eleven late in the series, when she got to be motherly.

HW: I found her reactions to be pretty realistic in hindsight. Except for a handful of people, it seemed that the rest of the town had quite a laid-back attitude to the strange goings-on, which, besides two disappearances, also included a killing, perpetrated by the good people at Hawkins. And Ryder's craziness led to one of the better scenes in the entire series, where she used the Christmas lights to communicate with her missing son. That had a big payoff.

Mentioning Hawkins makes me think of Matthew Modine's character, the sinister Dr. Martin Brenner, who functions as the face of the *Stranger Things'* first season "Big Bad." His ruthlessness and manipulation of Eleven (seen in flashbacks) recalls the character of Rainbird from King's *Firestarter*. Like that character, he also is an employee of a black ops government organization. In *Firestarter,* that organization was known as The Shop. They too experimented with LSD and experimental drugs, ultimately creating the title character, Charlie McGee. They were also quick to descend on the scene in King's *The Tommyknockers*.

BV: The death of the cafe owner, written off as a suicide, was the "shit just got real" moment for me. That was when I realized this series wasn't going to pull any punches. I've been asked whether this series would be appropriate for kids. When I tally up the record—implied sex, kids swearing, kids in incredible danger, kids dying—I have to say that I think it's not what I'd show a ten-year-old. It's a tough call, but this is a dark, dark show, with some very intense moments.

The "suicide" investigation was also a chance to show a different side of Chief Hopper. He is a fascinating character—a pill-popping, hard-drinking womanizer who is a damned fine cop when he's called to action. Extremely observant, and it's not just a one-off. He figures out that the surveillance video of the night Will vanished was switched because of the missing rainfall.

I thought it was an interesting decision to delay the full details of his backstory until the climactic scene, where his quest in the Inside Out reverberated with the death of his daughter. It was a risky decision, in my opinion, because it slowed the pace of the contemporary story, but it's another instance where this show favored character over plot.

HW: That was indeed a sobering moment. I kept thinking that Hopper, played by David Harbour (who recently turned up in *Suicide Squad*), was exactly the kind of character who would have been played by David Carradine, had it actually been made in the '80s. Hopper also reminds me of a couple of small-town lawmen who appear in Stephen King's novels, namely George Bannerman and Alan Pangborn. Again, we circle back to the theory that *Stranger Things* feels as if it were scripted by King and directed by either Spielberg or John Carpenter (in Carpenter's case, because of his style and résumé, and because the score sounds a lot like one he might have created).

As to your comment about this being appropriate for kids, it's definitely at least a PG-13 type show, there are some genuinely tense and frightening moments here. But nothing gratuitous: they all served the overall story.

In the end, I thought *Stranger Things* was well conceived (by the up-and-coming Duffer Brothers) and well executed, a miniseries that embraced and built on its influences. The acting was top-notch and the special effects were adequate. I wholeheartedly recommend this to anyone who seeks a few hours of diversion, away from real-world horrors, such as the current presidential campaign. It certainly did well in Netflix's view, as they recently announced a second season.

BV: I enjoyed it enough to watch it twice within a four- or five-week period. It wasn't perfect—a couple of things were done strictly for plot reasons that didn't ring true. Will's older brother "just happened" to be out in the woods with his camera (taking pictures of what, exactly?), which put him in a position to spy on the teen party and serendipitously capture an image of the demigorgon. Also, Will would have made his situation a lot easier on everyone if he'd made his presence known to someone other than his mother. And how did the DOE/Hawkins produce such a convincing duplicate body? And did Nancy strike you as the kind of person who would willingly climb through a mysterious, icky hole at the base of a tree in the middle of the woods without at least waiting for James?

But those are relatively minor quibbles. I could easily cite many more moments that I thought were clever. Having Steve arrive at the house when Nancy and Jonathan were in the midst of their demigorgon hunt, for example: he has no idea what's going on, and his reactions were priceless. Or the brief moment of Nancy realizing that Eleven is wearing her clothes. Or the ever-so-on-the-nose Dolly Parton song that was playing in the surplus store when Nancy and Jonathan were shopping for gear. Or the Ouija board made from Christmas lights. I'm totally with you in recommending this series without reservation. And it will be interesting to see where they take it in the second season. They left a few dangling threads to follow up, and they've already released the first teaser trailer.

Terrors of the Natural World

S. T. Joshi

RICHARD GAVIN. *Sylvan Dread: Tales of Pastoral Darkness*. [N.p.]: Three Hands Press, 2016. 192 pp. ISBN: 978-1-945147-02-9: $34.95 hc. ISBN: 978-1-945147-00-5: $22.95 tpb.

For more than a decade, Canadian Richard Gavin has been quietly amassing an enviable reputation as an author of weird tales that fuse sensitivity to the strangeness inherent in landscape with a keen insight into human emotions, expressed in prose that provides its own sensuous pleasures all apart from the subject matter. The volume under review is his fifth story collection, following *Charnel Wine* (2004), *Omens* (2007), *The Darkly Splendid Realm* (2009), and *At Fear's Altar* (2014). Gavin has also written a volume of "esotericism," *The Benighted Path: Primeval Gnosis and the Monstrous Soul* (2015) and co-edited an anthology of occult fiction, *Penumbrae* (2015).

Sylvan Dread proclaims in its very title that Gavin will expatiate on terrors found in the (almost) untenanted wilderness, and its assemblage of tales long and short do not fail to deliver. This is terrain that many of the masters of weird fiction, from Algernon Blackwood ("The Willows") to Arthur Machen ("The White People") to H. P. Lovecraft ("The Whisperer in Darkness") to Ramsey Campbell (*The Darkest Part of the Woods*), have made their own, and Gavin provides his own unique insight into what can happen when human beings give themselves up to the tender mercies of the natural world.

Gavin is at his best when he portrays conflicted human beings yearning to escape the stifling artificialities of urban life but unprepared to deal with the terrors—real or imagined—presented by the non-human realm of nature. "Tending the Mists" introduces us to a pair of twins, Muni and Zelia, who venture to a remote region where a wedding is to take place. Muni notes that all the guests except the groom appear to be women. Is some hideous sacrifice about to take place—and is Muni herself to be a victim, with her sister suddenly transformed into a goddess? In "Thistle Latch," the narrator tells of a friend he had when he was a child—a boy with the significant name of Lattice Rayburn. When the narrator as an adult has a strange experience in the woods, he seems to realize that Rayburn may have been some sort of trigger that would allow nature to violate its own laws. This tale has a powerfully Blackwoodian atmosphere of terror and awe while yet remaining grimly original.

"Fume" introduces us to a curmudgeon named Clark, who as a permanent resident of the beach resort of Beech Point welcomes the departure of the summer people who flock there. When he comes upon a tent placed in an area where it is illegal to camp, he thinks there is a dead body inside—but it is in fact an effigy of some sort. He stamps on it—and a strange cloud (or "fume") bursts out, going down his throat. This sets the stage for a horrifying scenario where the natural world seems to have invaded Clark's own cottage. "Weaned on Blood"—written for an anthology called *Monk Punk* (2015), which I assume is a volume of horror stories about monks—tells of Brother Baldemar, a Trappist monk, who finds loathsome evidence that a woman from the nearby village is nursing a "stone baby"—a baby that had calcified in her womb, but is in some fashion alive and, worse still, seems to feed on blood. The culmination of this appalling tale has to be read to be believed.

"Tinder Row" seems to begin as a tale of urban horror, as it takes us to a remote dead-end street called Tinder Row where the protagonist, Reid, grew up. He meets an old school friend named Agnes after many years. Her life has been marred by tragedy, and out of sympathy Reid takes her to Tinder Row, where she leads him to a copse with a curious human-shaped clearing. What Gavin has done is to draw us insidiously from the comfort of city life to the wilderness that lurks all too close to it—and then he concludes the tale with a cosmic flourish that Lovecraft would have appreciated.

"The Stiles of Palemarsh" is one of Gavin's most successful fusions of emotional tension and supernatural horror. A Canadian named Ian Morrow comes to Wales for what he says is his honeymoon—but he is alone. Twisting his ankle on a jog, he stumbles into a farmhouse, where he claims to the owner that his fiancée, Cari, stood him up at the altar. When the farmer directs him to the road that would take him back to his hotel, Ian finds himself in the midst of bizarre terrors, including a loathsome hermaphroditic entity ("The thing's head was like an overstuffed yard-waste sack. Excess leaves were tugged free by the damp breeze and went flitting off like startled birds"). We later learn that it was Ian who deserted Cari, and as he becomes increasingly disoriented he knows that the future bodes ill both for himself and his former beloved.

The novelette that concludes the volume, "Mare's Nest," is endowed with a poignant atmosphere of agonizing melancholy that each paragraph augments. When a young woman (she remains nameless, as does her husband) receives some dire but unspecified diagnosis that appears to signal her imminent demise (we are led to assume a malignant and incurable cancer), she compels her husband, a sculptor, to carry through with the promise he had made to her if such a situation were to arise. For many pages we are tantalized by what the couple is actually planning: why does the man first make a papier-mâché figure of a gigantic mare, then spend virtually all his savings on an immense block of black granite? Clearly we are to understand that the woman is planning her own death—but what will the man's fate be? The ineluctable gloom that descends upon readers as they continue to read, almost against their will, this almost unbearably intense narrative is a triumph of weird atmosphere.

"A Cavern of Redbrick" tells of a boy, Michael, who comes upon a storage shed in a gravel pit with a strange girl (perhaps made of ice?) sitting on top of it. This bizarre scenario leads to a confrontation with his grandfather, who turns out to be quite other than what Michael thought he was. "Goatsbride" is a luminous prose-poem, although I am not at all clear on the actual thrust or direction of the tale.

Not every tale is entirely successful. The novelette "Primeval Wood" (borrowed from *The Darkly Splendid Realm*) opens with a luminous paragraph that demonstrates Gavin's mastery of evocative prose:

> Certain miracles are reserved for the wayward and the damned. For just as every paradise has its netherworld and each metropolis its slum, the miraculous has its averse kin. Most people pass through this world wholly oblivious to the aberrant blessings that haunt its borders. But there are individuals among us who, by karmic debt or some other cold twist of fate, lead lives that are hopelessly intertwined with this adumbrated reality, this misshapen plane of existence that thrums beneath the skin of the physical.

Magnificent! But while the tale develops a powerful sense of the bizarre as Neil, apparently deserted by his girlfriend, Kate, finds his mental stability increasingly disturbed by the realization that days have passed without his conscious awareness, the narrative devolves into merely a story of psychological aberration that does not fully account for all the weird elements that have been haphazardly thrown out.

"Wormwood Votaries" is an obscure story about a man named Langdon who as a child experienced some strange visions when he was ill. Beyond that, however, it is difficult to grasp the purpose or intent of the tale. In "The Old Pageant" we find a woman who returns with her fiancé to the cabin she had visited as a child, where her grandmother had played a strange game called the Old Pageant. But the story ends indecisively.

There are enough successes in *Sylvan Dread* to counteract the few lesser items. This volume will only add to Gavin's well-deserved reputation as a master of quiet, restrained horror—but horror that is no less intense and gripping by being expressed in prose of unflagging elegance and grace.

Ramsey's Rant: Remembering Kirby

Ramsey Campbell

Just received letter % you from Kirby McCauley—I must say I'm flattered, and strangely the parts of the story he most praises are those I more or less took for granted! Thus he singles out the use of a deserted church as a setting (which I would have thought hackneyed rather than original) and likes the method of "escape" by my protagonist—being knocked down by a car—since he remarks this shows that normal people were wont to pass through such a town without realizing what things occurred there. I'll write to him today, anyway. . . .

I wrote thus to August Derleth on 16 December 1962. So began one of the crucial correspondences, not to mention friendships, of my life. The tale referred to was my first professional publication, "The Church in High Street," and it was typical of Kirby to want to convey his admiration to its author. I was only sixteen, and this was the first fan letter I'd ever received. Subsequently my first book was to earn a missive from Alberto R. Runge, a South American who enclosed a copy of his impenetrable pamphlet *Obstructions to Herencies* [*sic*] and offered to distribute some of my propaganda (Lovecraftian, I must assume), and a letter from Leonard of Greenwich Village, praising my author photograph and hoping to see more of me (presumably along the lines of the photo he sent of himself draped in a Turkish towel)—but Kirby's are the letters that have left by far the deepest impression on my mind.

I lost them all, along with every letter Robert Aickman wrote me and a great many others I regret, more than half my life ago while moving house. They're still vivid in my memory—Kirby's painstaking script that covered both sides of every A4 sheet, often half a dozen of them. My replies were nowhere near as generously eloquent, but I hope at least they weren't curt. Perhaps Kirby took them as typically English. Among the many topics we discussed and in some cases argued passionately over were literature and films and politics (in the latter area we converged towards the centre over the decades). A few random representative memories . . . He hugely admired Max Ophuls and listed the director's great work *Letter from an Unknown Woman* as his favourite film (though on a first viewing of Fellini's *8½* he declared it was the best film he'd ever seen). He was a thorough romantic, rhapsodising not just over Goethe but films such as *Portrait of Jennie* and the work of Frank Borzage (*Three Comrades,* for instance, where he was very taken with the theme of male friendship—*Jules et Jim* also drew his praise in that regard). While he was fond of Hitchcock, he felt let down by *Psycho,* in which he saw a lapse of taste (the shower scene) and felt that the director had abandoned elegance—he was dismayed when Hitchcock proposed to set a film in a hotel kitchen, where a severed finger would show up in the food. Oddly enough, he had no time for Stanley Donen's stab at an elegant thriller, *Charade*. Often a letter would include what amounted to an essay on a favourite director, scrutinising any number of their films, whereas my responses were generally much terser (never rudely so, I hope). He praised Fritz Lang and eventually compared my characters to Lang's in their moral greyness. Although his politics were well to the right of mine, he regarded Eisenstein much more highly than I did then. (He admired the men who went to fight in Vietnam, not the protesters who demonstrated against the war.) He enthused at length over Isaac Bashevis Singer, the richness of his imagery, the vividness of detail, the vitality of his characters and narrative, and sent me Singer's books to demonstrate their merits. He often mailed me copies of his favourite works, especially film scores on vinyl—a selection of Korngold's lush romantic contributions, Prokofiev's concert version of *Alexander Nevsky,* Leonard Bernstein's powerful music for *On the Waterfront*—and items that I couldn't find in Britain, such as Roddy McDowall's reading of two Lovecraft tales, even if they were actively not to his taste (albums by the Fugs, for instance, then banned in Britain). He enthused about the Doors—the rock band—and bought me a copy of their album *Strange Days*.

In October 1965 he toured Britain for a week and asked me to join him as his travelling companion, all expenses paid. Occasionally we shared a bed, though in an altogether manly fashion. Once he terrified me by driving onto the wrong side of a dual carriageway by mistake (an understandable error, let me say: I've very rarely taken the wheel in countries where you drive on the right). "Did I frighten you?" he said with glee. After the tour I wrote to August Derleth that "Kirby and I covered much of the country, including (inevitably) the Severn Valley, where around midnight we checked into an inn right on the bank of the river, and in the morning were pleasantly disquieted to discover that the inn's sign depicted a goat" (but we failed to track down Errol Undercliffe in Brichester, although I mentioned our time spent around there in "The Franklyn Paragraphs"). I recall staying overnight in Stratford-upon-Avon, where we saw Olivier in Strindberg's *Dance of Death,* which Kirby admired, the play and the performances too. He was more of a theatregoer than I—that lack is mine still—and in the West End we caught an adaptation of Iris Murdoch's *A Severed Head*. Of course we also packed in films once we reached London, genially disagreeing over Buñuel's *Journal d'une femme de chambre,* which I esteemed but which audibly offended Kirby as soon as it brought in boot fetishism, and coming closer to agreement over *Wild Strawberries* (which led him to revalue Ingmar Bergman upwards to an extent) and *Les Enfants du Paradis,* whose screenplay Kirby judged to be the greatest in his experience. We both enthused about *The Sun Shines Bright,* which for me remains one of John Ford's most moving films. When we saw it at the National Film Theatre it engrossed a silently respectful audience;

who knows how it might be received there now? At some point we discussed romantic relationships, and Kirby apparently declared "I'd get married tomorrow if the right girl came along." Alas, this was never to be.

In 1966 Kirby seems to have gone incommunicado for a while. In March Derleth wrote to me "A propos McCauley & [Charles] Swoope—I've not heard from either for a year or so, I should guess. I suppose they are only typical of many young fans—as they grow older, other interests assert themselves, and they fall away from Arkham House & the macabre generally." Happily, Kirby was back in touch with me in April, and the following year he and Derleth sent me heartening supportive letters when my brief engagement to a girl collapsed (though soon enough I saw that the collapse had been the best outcome for us both). I was hugely grateful to them, and I sometimes wonder if August realised when he later purchased "Napier Court" that it dealt with that disastrous relationship in fictionalised form. Kirby did, and so did J. Vernon Shea, to whom he passed the carbon of the typescript. JVS thought the tale showed I would have been no great catch for my ex-fiancée, which had rather been the point of the relentlessly accurate characterisation.

I believe, though sadly I can't confirm it with any documents, that it was in 1968 we toured Europe. I wish more memories had stayed with me, though most of the peripheral details in my tale "The Lost" derive from the German section of that trip, where I gorged myself at the Hofbräuhaus in Munich and appalled Kirby by drinking a stein of beer with my breakfast wurst before we boarded the train to—I forget where, though perhaps Budapest. No doubt it's typical of writers, or at any rate of me, that I still recall seeing a German in a crowd with his small son on his shoulders and instantly reworking this as an image of a totem pole (not actually seeing this but finding the words and being conscious of the process). We ended our European tour in Paris, where I for one was delighted to see people queuing round the block for a revival of Leo McCarey's 1935 comedy *Ruggles of Red Gap* and to join them. Back in London we visited Robert Aickman in Gower Street, an encounter described in my reminiscence of him.

I believe this meeting was crucial to Kirby's decision to become a literary agent, having observed that many British writers of the weird were unrepresented in America. Robert was one of the first, and I was another. Kirby felt he couldn't properly represent his clients from his home in Minneapolis, and so he moved to New York. As well as developing his British stable, he had a keen eye for new American talent that the more established agencies ignored, and he also revived the careers of writers from the pulps he loved—Manly Wade Wellman was one such grateful beneficiary. In the case of poor Frank Belknap Long, Kirby eventually supplemented his client's income out of his own pocket. He involved himself gently but persuasively in quite a few of his authors' creative processes: George R. R. Martin has written of how Kirby persuaded him and Lisa Tuttle to develop their Windhaven novella into a novel, and in our first professional years he kept encouraging me to write a novel until at last I gave in, to my great advantage.

In 1975 he was the driving force behind the first World Fantasy Convention, of which he was the chairman. As an admirer of *Weird Tales* rather than of Campbell's *Unknown* (which I believe he found overall too lightweight and irreverent), he invited as many writers as he could from the former magazine. He also brought in many of the younger generation—inevitably, quite a few of his clients—and flew me over from Liverpool. I'd scarcely arrived at his apartment at 220 East 26th Street when he whisked me out again, not to eat (though I'm sure we did that) but to cross town to a showing of *The Texas Chainsaw Massacre,* which he couldn't wait for me to experience. He chortled at every shock and revelled in my own starts of alarm. Like George R. R. and many another Pimlico Agency client, I slept on the couch in Kirby's apartment, next to a radiator whose piercing hiss rivalled that of the one in *Eraserhead*. During my stay he recommended a new horror writer he thought I would like, and I certainly did. I still have the paperback I bought on his advice, with the embossed face and the discreet drop of blood on the otherwise black glossy cover.

In the late '70s Jenny and I stayed with our friends Gary and Uschi Klüpfel outside Munich while I researched *The Parasite*. Kirby proved to be in Europe and bought us dinner, where Jenny's amusement at the name of an item on the menu—Gypsy Spit, presumably a species of kebab—won his affection. He accompanied us on our return to London and booked us into an expensive hotel for the night, under the names of Errol and Hyacinth Undercliffe.

He was my host on several later visits to New York, and in the

'80s I enjoyed his hospitality in his splendid lofty apartment at 425 Park Avenue South. Those were the days when cocaine was regarded as (I quote) the champagne of drugs, before the grislier effects became widely known. At least we knew enough to sluice our nostrils, but I never found the substance especially rewarding, and suspected it of only doing its full job once you were addicted. Parsimony as much as wisdom saved me from following that route.

In later years we were in touch mostly by phone. Kirby would call up and deliver the equivalent of one of his old letters, full of his latest enthusiasms or rediscovered ones and punctuated by his trademark chuckle. The calls became less frequent once he suffered a fall in the shower, but whenever they came he hadn't changed, except perhaps by edging slightly further to the left in some ways. I recall his reminiscing about our old political spats, when (as he put it) we were full of piss and vinegar.

Alas, we rather lost touch in his last years. He died in August 2014, a little over a year earlier than the fortieth anniversary of that first World Fantasy Convention he chaired. I should hope that if he'd still been alive, he would have been a special guest at the event in Saratoga Springs. I was supposed to be one in order to receive an award, but an injury kept me in England. As far as I could see, the programme included no tribute to Kirby, and so I celebrated him and his sister Kay (who took over the agency, and still runs it) in my acceptance speech by electronic link. Without the two of them I would certainly not be the writer I am, and perhaps even unheard of.

That fortieth convention felt very much like the end of an era. David Hartwell, another of the prime movers behind the World Fantasy events, died early the following year. He'd administered the awards, and at Saratoga he announced (unheard by me) that Gahan Wilson's bust of Lovecraft was no longer to be used as the statuette. I've subsequently wondered how many of those who signed the online petition to have it removed had previously cared about the award or even heard of it. I was proud to receive it in its original form, and I still recall how Kirby chuckled at the sight of so many inimitable Gahan Wilson images lined up behind the podium in 1975. How would he have reacted to the new opprobrium? Would he have kept his sense of humour, which seems in short supply elsewhere? Wherever he is now, may he be mirthful. Perhaps in due course he and I may reunite to watch a complete print of Orson

Welles' *The Magnificent Ambersons*. I suspect that would be heaven for us both.

Psychosexual Syzygy: Checking in at the Bates Motel

Gavin Callaghan

Bates Motel, Seasons 1 through 5 (A&E, 2013–17).

The *Psycho* myth continues. And it certainly is a myth, just like the Greek *Oresteia* or the *Oedipus* tragedies before it. A young man and his mother indulge in a forbidden love; the son become jealous, kills the mother, then goes mad from guilt, and in his madness robs her grave and finally *becomes* his mother. For some reason, the United States of America recognized something of itself in this bizarre myth—something that made *Psycho* the most successful of Hitchcock's films, and which supported a string of five movie sequels, two literary ones, and a continuing succession of nonfiction books on the topic.

Robert Bloch probably did not know he was creating a great American tragedy in 1959, when he concocted the weird story of Mrs. Bates and her sadistic son from the raw materials supplied by the Ed Gein murders in Wisconsin. Bloch's interest in the case was purely Lovecraftian. In his 1960 article "The Shambles of Ed Gein," Bloch invokes H. P. Lovecraft twice—both times with regard to Lovecraft's famous opening lines from "The Picture in the House": "Searchers after horror haunt strange places. . . . But the true epicure in the terrible [. . .] esteems most of all the ancient, lonely farmhouse of backwoods New England . . ." The basic outlines of *Psycho* mirror "The Picture in the House" almost exactly: a solitary traveler seeks relief from a heavy downpour in an abandoned-looking residence. Both travelers meet with a perverse/insane individual in the place they turn to for shelter. There are hints of cannibalism, sadism, sexual perversity, and murder. In both stories, incongruously archaic architectural elements are used to create a sense of unease and mystery (Mary Crane is especially amazed by the old-fashioned parlor and kitchen in the Bates house, while her sister Lila is equally amazed by the atavistic-looking bathroom. Lovecraft's Old Man, meanwhile, seems to be a living relic from the colonial era.) Both stories invoke primitive native rituals and rites to symbolize a modern-day resurgence of sadism and perversity (via the Old Man's book on African cannibals in "The Picture in the House" and Norman Bates's various books on South Seas savages and the Incas in *Psycho*). Indeed, Lovecraft's pointed use of *an illustration* in a book to denote and embody horror will later be echoed almost precisely in Bloch's novel (in a scene quietly replicated in Hitchcock's movie), in which Lila Crane finds "a nondescript assortment of untitled volumes, poorly bound" on the bottom shelf in Norman's bedroom. Taking out one "at random," Lila is shocked to see what Bloch calls an "almost pathologically pornographic" illustration that "leaped out at her." (Does it also show African natives butchering peoples' bodies, like the Old Man's cherished book—or is it some more modern equivalent?)

In fact, although the Gein murders are often cited in connection to *Psycho,* its basic plot seems to have been percolating in Bloch's imagination long before the world had ever heard of Gein in 1957. In 1952 in *Weird Tales,* for example, Bloch had written a splendid short story entitled "Lucy Comes to Stay," in which (SPOILER ALERT) the murderer turns out to be a split-personality named Lucy who lives in the mind of the narrator, Vi. Numerous elements from *Psycho* (and *Bates Motel*) are already here, *in utero:* the blackouts, the alcoholism, and the final destruction of the murderer's self-identity. Indeed, the frightening dialogues between Vi and Lucy seem to prefigure, almost exactly, the various conversations between Norman and his fictional *alter ego* in *Bates Motel*—with Mother doing her best to undermine and destabilize the sanity of her "son," all in the guise of protecting him. The only thing that the Gein murders seems to have added to Bloch's basic plot was the theme of transvestitism.

As early as the 1930s, in a short satirical article entitled "A Visit with H. P. Lovecraft," published in a fanzine called the *Science-Fantasy Correspondent,* Bloch was toying with the same ideas later found in *Psycho*. In this brief tale, Bloch gives an entirely imaginary—and very funny—account of a supposed visit to the home of Lovecraft, who is depicted very much like the bearded, archaic cannibal in "The Picture in the House." Indeed, this Lovecraft wears nothing else *besides* this beard—he had "promised my mother" that he would never shave—so that it now completely covers his body and face. The story also ends very much like "Picture," with Lovecraft pulling aside his beard to reveal a set of fangs, with which he proceeds to eat the startled narrator.

Although Bloch made a point, on several occasions, to deny that Lovecraft was in any way "sick"—or at least no more sick than other great writers such as Kafka, Poe, Wilde, or Shakespeare—it is not hard to see a little of Lovecraft in Bloch's portrait of the disturbed Norman Bates. Both men were teetotalers (although Bates was a secret alcoholic). Both men were also the sole son of a dominating mother, who raised them after their fathers' disappearance (Lovecraft's father went insane and was hospitalized, while Bates's father simply "ran off"). As Bloch himself observed of Lovecraft:

> . . . his mother survived until 1921, but her own mental instability increased as the family fortunes declined . . . it was his neurotic mother who labeled him peculiar and 'protected' him from contact with other youngsters.

Like Norman, Lovecraft's personality encompassed wide contradictions and extremes: an overgrown child who loved ice cream on the one hand, he was also a cosmic philosopher whose vision comprehended vast sweeps of time and space. As Bloch observes, Norman "wasn't her little boy anymore. He was a grown man, a man who studied the secrets of time and space and mastered the secrets of dimension and being." Indeed, the outré contents of Bates's bookshelf could very well have been lifted from a catalogue of Lovecraft's own library, even to the detail of including Dr. Margaret Murray's *Witch-Cult in Western Europe*—one of Lovecraft's favorite anthropological texts.

The connection isn't as improbable as it may seem. After all, Lovecraft and Bloch occasionally used each other as protagonists in other horror stories. Lovecraft figured in Bloch's "The Shambler from the Stars" (a title later re-used in "The Shambles of Ed Gein"), while Bloch appears (as Robert Blake) in Lovecraft's "The Haunter of the Dark." Bloch's creation of Norman Bates can perhaps be read as a later, and heretofore unidentified, appearance of Lovecraft in Bloch's work—a critical/satirical depiction of the darker side of Lovecraft's unfortunate maternal situation.

Norman Bates's final transformation into "Mother" at the end of

Bloch's story, too—completely effacing his own Norman-identity—could almost be read as a more mundane, psychologically based version of the body-switching theme in Lovecraft's "The Thing on the Doorstep," in which Edward Derby's body is dominated, and his personality supplanted, by that of his sinister "wife" Asenath (who is herself a basically surrogate for Edward's dead mother). Indeed, it is arguably this same fear (and fascination) with emasculation and domination by the feminine that so disturbs Lovecraft's hero Delapore in "The Rats in the Walls"—who writes shiveringly of "the hideous rites of the Eastern god [Atys], whose worship was so mixed with that of Cybele"—rites that involved ritualized castration during an ecstatic frenzy. As we shall see, it may be that something of the same furtive fascination likewise underlies the continuing American interest in the myth of *Psycho;* and that in this horrifying vision of masculinity unmanned and transformed by the feminine, we are witnessing a deeper transformation within our culture itself.

Like most myths, of course, the *Psycho* story was the creation of many hands—first Bloch, and then Hitchcock, who, with screenwriter Joseph Stefano, transformed Norman Bates from an unshaven, overweight, bespectacled, middle-aged alcoholic to the smiling, friendly boy next door.

Although some have claimed that Hitchcock's masterpiece is not a horror film, it certainly had an incalculable impact upon the genre of horror, as it did on so many other aspects of American life and film. As David Thomson convincingly argues in his book *The Moment of Psycho* (2009), nothing was quite the same after Norman Bates's sinister secret was revealed. The heroine did not always survive; detectives did not know all; and the nice young hero could harbor a monster inside.

And while it is true that all these elements were already to be found in Bloch's novel, Hitchcock only chose this novel for adaptation because its noir contours represented the same deeply held point of view that informed nearly all of Hitchcock's movies. Whether the novelist was Robert Bloch or Patricia Highsmith, each novel that Hitchcock adapted seemed to share a similar worldview about the secret prevalence of sin and the hidden undertow of evil that seems to flow behind the scenes of American consumer existence, ever ready to suck down those whom luck or fate has foredoomed to destruction.

This seems to have been less an economic or social view of

Hitchcock's than a basic metaphysical one. As Peter Conrad observes in *The Hitchcock Murders* (2000), he once rather egoistically "described the deity as a maker of thrillers, a would-be Hitchcock, and argued that 'when God keeps the future hidden, He is saying that things would be very dull without suspense.'"

*

The TV series *Bates Motel* is firmly situated within this ironic, Hitchcockian worldview (later explored so well by filmmakers such as David Lynch): a secret American world of true crime, desperate noir robberies, drug dealing, and gun running. It is a shadowy realm whose moral ambiguity allows a secret murderer like Norman Bates to grow and thrive within the corrupt community of White Pine Bay. I think that Alfred Hitchcock would have been very proud of this show. Its producers, Kerry Ehrin and Carlton Cuse, literally got everything right—at least, for the first four seasons (about which more below).

Bates Motel succeeds as noir. It succeeds as a mystery. It succeeds as a thriller. It succeeds as drama (although veering, at times, a little too closely to soap opera, with an overt reliance on coincidence as a plot device, resulting in numerous dangling plot-threads). It succeeds as irony, and as a pitch-black dark comedy. It succeeds as tragedy and as a modern version of an American myth. And most unexpectedly (especially after Gus Van Sant's remake debacle), it succeeds as a worthy tribute and follow-up to the original *Psycho* (indeed, in some ways, it is superior to Hitchcock's *Psycho*).

I admit that I was not particularly looking forward to this series. Advertised as being "from the producers of *Lost*," I feared *Bates Motel* might be more of the same, using the mere name of Bloch and Hitchcock's creation as a vehicle for hip modernity and catchphrase references. Indeed, the fact that this series was advertised as a *prequel* to *Psycho* with a *modern-day setting* (a paradox of the most puzzling kind) led me to fear the worst: that the story would jettison its very soul in an attempt to be "hip," contemporary, relevant, or current. Like so many others, I asked: *Why not shoot it as a period-piece?*

But after all, Hitchcock had not filmed *Psycho* as a period-piece; and to do so now would rob the drama of any reality or immediacy. (Again, one thinks of Van Sant's misguided remake.) This fact—plus the show's much greater length—enables *Bates Motel* to explore

Bloch's story with a richness and depth that even Hitchcock could never have accomplished.

The look of the show, too, is impressive, and as intricate and deep as the writing. Cinematography, production design, casting: all reflect a finely tuned and subtle touch, full of long establishing shots, deep focus, moody locations, and slow takes. In a modern-day film industry of frenetic Michael Bay–style editing and pointless jump-scares, the slow, deliberate pacing of this show is especially notable, and a welcome return to traditional methods of storytelling. (Unfortunately, as we shall see below, the pacing in Season Five has become a little *too* slow and deliberate.) *Bates Motel* is a show that is not afraid to take its time: from the slow camera-crawl outside the strip club visited by Norman's half-brother Dylan (Max Thieriot) in Season One to the long and largely wordless sequence in which Dylan takes his younger brother on a motorbike ride through the countryside.

Most of all, *Bates Motel* succeeds as a character portrait of one remarkable and unforgettable woman: Norma Bates (Vera Farmiga)—who is perceived by the citizens of White Pine Bay as just another mere daffy or kooky housewife (one character calls her a "nut"), but whose character plumbs unknown depths of horror—a tragedy only increased by her inevitable fate at the end of Season Four: to be murdered and mummified by her own son. In the original film, Mother lives on only as a shadow, and aside from her corpse we never really see her—except as she lives on in the form of her demented child. *Bates Motel,* however, succeeds in bringing this formerly voiceless corpse to life.

To be sure, Norma's tragedy (as is usually the case) is entirely self-made and begins with her stubborn refusal to alert law enforcement after Norman's impulsive murder of his father, Sam. This first murder lays the groundwork for all the others, until eventually Norma's situation literally becomes a pit, swallowing up everything around her.

Like most people singled out for persecution by the gods, Norma's cardinal sin lies in her attempt to forestall or outwit the Fate decreed for her and her son—namely, that they would be separated by time and events. (Later, Norman's own sin would be rooted in a similarly godlike attempt to forestall change—an encroachment of the human upon the divine, which cannot be allowed.) One of the rules of tragedy is that the gods are jealous: in this case, jealous that Norma would attempt to create her own small, domestic version of paradise with her son (a perpetual "tea party," as her estranged son Dylan sarcastically calls it). In Season One, Norma sets up her son's bedroom right next to her own, with an adjoining door between them—like a young girl preparing for an extended slumber party. Later, in Season Two, Norma revealingly refers to Norman as her "sister," during a discussion with her doctor. The subtle feminization implied by Norma's actions in this regard is obvious, and as we all know Norman will later take it all a little too far. (As Dylan exclaims at one point to Norman: "She's *ruined* you.") Sheriff Romero, uncannily perceptive as he is, sizes up the situation right away on the very night he first meets Norma, when he comments upon the weird similarity between the names of Norma and Norman. Mother and son are too close.

By the time Season Three comes around, the writing is on the wall for Norma. It is difficult to keep track of the number of references to "fate" and approaching death in Season Three. And by the end of Season Four, Norma's stubborn refusal to admit that her son is dangerous leads to her inevitable murder—the tragedy made all the more painful by the fact that she had numerous tantalizing opportunities to escape from this self-made trap. (If she had simply married the kind, wealthy George Heldens in Season Two, for instance, everything would have been fine.) The entirety of the masterful fourth season was essentially an extended *conte cruel,* briefly elevating Norma out of her pit and granting her a brief glimpse of possible escape—only to snatch it irrevocably away at the final instant.

As of this writing, we are now roughly through the first half of the final season of the show, with only a few episodes left to go. And although the show's producers are keeping mum about the eventual fate of Norman Bates (Freddie Highmore), the gradual disintegration of his life seems to be essentially following the same pattern as that of his mother. Indeed, everything about Norman is basically a dark caricature of Norma. From his very first appearance the very first episode, every word he says is a distorted echo of what she has said. (Alert viewers should especially take note of Norman's curious use of the word "we" whenever he speaks of himself—symbolic of the schizophrenic divide within.) Norman is essentially two people:

himself and "Mother," a murderous and sadistic version of Norma constructed within his subconscious mind.

As with any myth, numerous changes inevitably occurred with each successive version of *Psycho,* from film to film, and from novel to novel. Some of these changes, as in the misguided *Bates Motel* (1987) TV movie, have been for the worse (although I truly have a soft spot for the kindhearted nostalgia of this failed pilot). In the new *Bates Motel,* however, these changes have been mostly judicious—and some of them brilliant.

The show's creators were actually following the lead of Joseph Stefano himself (who did the same thing in *Psycho IV*) in transforming Norma Bates from a domineering old crone into a beautiful, vibrant younger woman. But *Bates Motel* greatly improves upon this basic conceit, presenting us with a woman who is essentially a localized version of the Mother Goddess: the untamed and dangerous manifestation of primal chaos. Erich Neuman called her the "Terrible Mother"—whose various manifestations include such vampiric demonesses as the Lamia, Lilith, and Medusa. (As a puzzled Sheriff Romero [Nestor Carbonell] tells Norma, "Chaos seems to surround you. I'm not sure why.") And spinning around this central zone of chaos are the numerous males caught up in her treacherous orbit—beginning in childhood with her brother, Caleb, and later expanding to include her two sons Dylan and Norman. Even the usually stolid, emotionless Sheriff Romero eventually succumbs to her charms—transformed, in Season Five, into a crazed killer, embarking on a relentless quest of vengeance on her behalf. As Caleb tells Dylan, "Yeah, well nobody gets passed that [i.e., loving Norma.]"

Meanwhile Norman Bates, in this new version of the story, seems to owe much more to the sad case of Adam Lanza (the autistic teenager who murdered his mother, before going on to slaughter dozens of schoolchildren), than to the cannibalistic Ed Gein. (Highmore even closely resembles Lanza in appearance.) He also seems far younger than Anthony Perkins in *Psycho* (Season One begins with Norman as a junior in high school), and he lacks Perkins' tall, thin angularity. This actually works in the character's favor; no one would suspect this small, unremarkable individual to be so dangerous. Men like Sam Loomis bully the diminutive Norman with impunity; and when Norman tries to intimidate the near seven-foot tall mountain-man Chick Hogan (a confederate in Norman's crimes, who seems to be loosely-based upon Ed Gein's mysterious cohort, "Gus"), he needs the aid of a staircase to do it. Women, especially, see Norman as essentially harmless—which makes him that much more successful as a predator. (As a perceptive Marion Crane asks him, when she sees all the creepy stuffed animals decorating his office: "Are you a hunter?") Norman is essentially like the tiger in Blake's poem, "Tyger, Tyger"—unfathomable, intricate and dangerous.

Ultimately, the divide within Norman's mind, between good/decent/sensitive boy and amnesiac/unconscious/sadistic killer, is the same as that in the surrounding town of White Pine Bay. The larger world around him reflects the same basic contradiction between beauty and evil, peace and violence, domestic calm and the death which sustains it with every meal. Norman symbolizes and exposes this larger duality. In the opening episode of Season One ("First You Dream, Then You Die"), a beautiful girl named Bradley Martin tells Norman that she sees him as "special". But Bradley herself is just as corrupt—and blind—as the world around them, whose blindness nurtures Norman's secret evil.

One of the more interesting changes in this version of the myth, is making Norman Bates a fan of pornographic *manga* comics, featuring bondage and sadism. (Norman finds one such volume hidden in one of the hotel rooms and later spends his spare time in his bedroom examining it with fascination.) In the original *Psycho,* as we have seen, Norman is also a fan of pornography—not to mention more "classical" sources of sadism and perversion, such as Sade's *Justine*. This use of pornographic *manga* is also emblematic of the difficulties in updating *Psycho* for modern audiences, since such images are nowadays not at all shocking (at least for younger people). As the straitlaced Emma tells Norman, she has seen *manga* that is "a lot steamier than this." Only *Norman* regards the images in the book as in any way deviant—a subtle transformation of values that will later come to the fore in the middle of Season Five, in which Norman is shocked and horrified to find that he (in his guise of Mother) has been visiting a gay bar during his various recurring blackouts.

Equally ingenious was to have Norma's husband, Romero, survive the attempt on her life. (In the original *Psycho,* Norman murders his mother and her lover, Joe Considine, together "in bed.") Instead, *Bates Motel* (in a further nod to the noir genre) has chosen to leave him alive, to embark on his quest for revenge against his stepson.

Indeed, whereas Norma was the Terrible Mother, Romero is a perfect embodiment of the father archetype, the thunder god of vengeance and retribution—a fact that only serves to aggravate Norman's labyrinthine Oedipal complexes. (As Norma once tells Romero, he's "the big daddy of White Pine Bay.")

*

In this final season of the show, however, some of the changes have been curious, to the point of revisionism. The most obvious and controversial change—though hardly the most significant in this regard—has been the casting of Rhianna as murder-victim Marion Crane (played by Janet Leigh in the original *Psycho*). While I can well understand the controversy, I believe it works in this instance. As in Hitchcock's *Vertigo,* in which Jimmy Stewart's dead love seems to return from the dead, Madeline Loomis is introduced in Season Five as a sort of Norma redivivus (albeit slightly younger). With a name derived from Roderick's sister in Poe's "Fall of House of Usher" (who apparently dies but is in fact buried alive), she almost resembles a reanimated double of Norma, right down to her facial expressions and body gestures. As such, it greatly helps to have Marion played by as different a physical type as possible.

More bizarre, and shocking, is the strange reluctance of the show's creators to depict Norman in his garb as "Mother," actually murdering people while in a wig and dress. (Norman *has* appeared in blouse and wig, but not while killing.) So far we are seven episodes into Season Five, with only three left to go, and we have yet to see this iconic image; instead, we see Norman murdering people while in his normal street clothes.

Perhaps the creators of *Bates Motel* are saving this potent and iconic image for the very end—as Roger Ebert once argued the original *Psycho* should have done. (Ebert disliked the long expository psychological explanation at the end.) But if not, then they are taking the slow and deliberate pacing of the program a little *too* far. The finale of Season Four took us to the very pinnacle of insanity; Season Five was supposed to be the moment of the final plunge, showing the complete submerging of Norman's self beneath his homicidal Mother-half.

But now, unaccountably, the creators seem to be drawing back, perhaps in preparation for some final act of self-redemption. Two of

Norman's victims this season were unlikable characters (one was actually killed in self-defense), while another, innocent victim (Dr. Edwards) was killed off-screen—almost as if the creators are trying to remake Norman Bates in the image of such deplorable serial killer anti-heroes as Hannibal or Dexter.

Were the show's creators simply worried that such an image (later repeated in such films as de Palma's *Dressed to Kill,* Ken Russell's *Crimes of Passion,* and Demme's *Silence of the Lambs*) is now too clichéd?

The climax of horror at the end of the original *Psycho* was its violation of dark and forbidden taboos—most notably, gender roles and transvestitism, but also incest and necrophilia. The final shot in the basement (before the final dissolve to the denouement at the sheriff's office) was like a distorted American family portrait (an idea later revisited in films like *Texas Chainsaw Massacre*). The dead mother is seated in her rocking chair as if upon a throne, vacant, desiccated, and decayed, but still a potent, living force, looming large over the proceedings, her shriveled face twisted into an awful grin, as if in ironic mirth at her handiwork. Beside her stands Lila Crane (Vera Miles), Mother's living embodiment and a representative of refined American domesticity, who looks on in horror as she watches the approach of her deranged doppelgänger, Norman Bates. And finally we have Norman in his guise of Mother, with his "cheap wig" and ill-fitting dress, rushing into the room with his glinting knife. He is *the thing that should not be*—the dead mother revived in the body of son, the crazed worshipper of Cybele, castrated in the name of Atys, his face frozen in unholy glee.

So what do we encounter in Season Five? A new Norman Bates—strangely akin to the new Superman, who no longer rescues people or wears red underwear. A Norman who murders while dressed in male clothing, and who kills bad, or at least morally questionable, men. Is this really Norman Bates? As David Lynch once observed about the changes made during second season of *Twin Peaks,*, in an interview with Chris Rodley:

> ... Cooper ceased to be 100 per cent Cooperesque for me. He got these flannel shirts and stuff! Some people liked it. So you say, "Yes, I'm glad in a way, and in another way I'm really sorry because a guy that's too much like me cannot sustain that intense interest or

dream." He's got to be specific. Cooper is a certain way. It's necessary. If you start seeing the Queen of England going around in a Volkswagen or something, it doesn't make it. It's gotta be a Rolls-Royce. That's what you want.

Partly, such changes are probably a sensible reflection of or response to larger changes in our culture. How can Norman's transformation into his homicidal Mother be in any way terrifying, in a modern society where, both legally or culturally, differences in gender have been minimized? Ephraim Waite now *is* Asenath Waite.

The depiction of the marijuana industry in the show (used to symbolize moral ambiguity) was swallowed by much the same trap. *Bates Motel* was produced right on the cusp of marijuana legalization. And after the passing of several nationwide referenda to legalize medical marijuana, many of the plotlines involving drugs were rather abruptly dropped from the show. Here again, a central cultural change undermined the atmosphere of the program.

The bar scene in episode 5.5 ("Dreams Die First") is emblematic of such changes. Tracing Mother's movements after one of his blackouts, Norman discovers that he has unknowingly been visiting an establishment called The White Horse. The crowd in the bar seems completely accepting of Norman in his role of Mother; in fact, they seem surprised to see him *not* wearing his wig and a dress. "That's a new look for you," one of the bar patrons observes. It's an odd but also a very clever reversal. Instead of Vera Miles being stunned at the final revelation of Mother—it is now *Norman himself* who recoils in horror from the sudden revelation of his own secret homosexual life.

Significantly, the bar itself is presented as warm, welcoming, and friendly, not at all a scary place. This was intentional. As the show's creators told *TVLine.com,* they wanted the bar to have

> . . . an edgy vibe but not a scary vibe. . . . There's a sense that everybody is pretty cool there and that anything goes and that people all kind of know each other. There are probably all kinds of different things happening in that bar. [It's] an open minded bar, let's put it that way.

In other words—it's basically a microcosm of the current state of post-millennial culture, at least in the West.

Hitchcock's Norman scared the whole United States of America; the new Norman scares only himself.

This depiction of Mother's secret homosexual life is also a rather strange divergence from the original myth. Norman is presented as virginal in the book, and as being very repressed in Hitchcock's film. The idea that Norman was gay in the original *Psycho* seems to have been due more to carryover from actor Anthony Perkins's tortured private life than to the character created by Bloch. As Christopher Nickens observes:

> Later, when Norman climbs the stairs of the Bates house to bring his mother's remains down to the cellar, his gait as he walks up the staircase is just the slightest bit swishy. Was Tony offering a subtle hint regarding his character's sexuality?

I might have been willing to accept a gay Norman Bates on *Bates Motel,* if it had been adequately set up in the story beforehand (see George Romero's chilling vampire movie *Martin* [1978] for some good examples of such sexual ambiguity). But this sudden revelation in episode 5.5 seems to contradict what we have seen before in Seasons One to Four, which show Norman to be sexually fixated on a very specific type of woman: loose and troubled (Blair Watson, Annika Johnson, Cody Brennan, the stripper Athena)—what Norma used to call "slutty" or "sex-crazed" women, and what Norman (rather oddly) calls "nice girls." Marion Crane is of this type precisely.

Unfortunately, Norman's desires in this direction are also inextricably bound up with an insatiable sadism and Oedipal bloodlust—what Norman calls a whole "other part of me." In the episode "What's Wrong with Norman?," for example, Bates suffers a public blackout after his bondage fantasies about his pretty teacher dissolve into a vision of his own mother, tied and bound. In Season Four, the sexual desires aroused by a stripper resolve into images of stabbing, blood, and death. In Season Two, on the other hand, we watched as Norman dodged a gay pass made at him at summer beach party.

One also has to ask: is this really the sort of place that Mother, the sexual-sadist, would frequent? Would Mother really be found in such a *friendly, open* environment as this bar? Given her penchant for blood and violence, wouldn't a bondage club of some sort, catering to a far more dangerous or shady clientele, have been more appropriate? Or perhaps Mother would stay at home, surfing evil websites dedicated to blood and death, or graduating from bondage manga to watching evil DVDs like *Tumbling Doll of Flesh*.

In my opinion, it would have been better simply not to show Mother/Norman having any sexual outlet at all; instead, his only release would be in blood and death—exactly as Seasons One to Four seemed to indicate.

The one other great change with regard to the new Marion Crane (SPOILER ALERT) is Norman's *letting her survive,* and instead killing her cheating boyfriend, Sam Loomis. If Norman lets Marion Crane live, is he really Norman Bates any longer?

In this sense, the "Marion" episode is as pivotal to this series as the original shower-scene was to the original *Psycho*. Sure, it's *nice* that he let her go. But then, that was the horror of it—that a nice girl died. At this point, the divergence from the source material has become a rewriting. So then we must ask: revised for what reason, and according to what underlying intention?

True, the show's creators were wise to change the shower-scene: simply copying the original would, again, have been to fall into Gus Van Sant's trap. But to change things this way: it's becoming Norman Bates-lite. A feel-good Norman.

Don't get me wrong: the episode "Marion" is a minor masterpiece of plotting, as it depicts Norman's slow but certain disintegration throughout the episode, from outer calm to complete, shivering turmoil. From the symbolic apple of knowledge that Mother offers Norman to the spilled cup of wine that spells doom for Sam, it is horrifying and chilling as we witness the inevitable onset of Norman's recurring, homicidal rage (his final return to murder accompanied by Roy Orbison's "Crying" is a brilliant touch). And, just as in Stefano's original script, we witness Norman's unexpected and touching connection with Marion—both of them caught in their private traps, both of them afraid (rightly, as it turns out) that their respective loves, for Mother and Sam Loomis, are not real.

The victim is not a woman this time, however, but a man—one who (the creators seem to be suggesting) somehow deserves this fate. In the original *Psycho,* Marion's shower has been likened to a baptism, a ritual cleansing of sorts. She has decided to return home and give back the money she has stolen. There is a sense of happiness and hope. Cut short, of course, by an act of madness.

In the new version, Sam also regrets his past actions, telling Marion that he wants to be with her and leave his wife. But his regret is somehow less believable than Marion's in the original film. And his shower seems less an act of renewal than a futile attempt to wipe off a stain with which he has been branded—in this case, the wine thrown by his wife, Madeline.

Norman, meanwhile, is apparently driven to kill Sam by the same Oedipal rage that first impelled him to murder his own father. As we watch Mother (taking a page from Lady Macbeth) goading Norman on to the murder, her face seems to grow out from Norman's profile, like a schizophrenic Janus—telling Norman that the philandering Sam treated the women around him "like trash."

But is this rather late-in-the-day recasting of Norman as a defender of women's rights really convincing? Especially given that he has previously bashed out poor Bradley Martin's brains against a rock and asphyxiated his own mother for daring to have a life of her own?

The placing of a man in the shower, too, is not such a great innovation. After all, Stefano had a brief male shower-scene in *Psycho IV*—and even the *Bates Motel* TV movie featured Bud Cort in a shower scene.

In my opinion, a better way to revise the shower-scene, in keeping with the spirit of the original film, would have been to:

1) keep Marion as the victim;

2) show Norman and Mother arguing before the murder, as Norman struggles to prevent what "she" is about to do;

3) fade to black, as Norman experiences yet another mental blackout (or is knocked out by Mother);

4) fade-in to Norman in a daze, waking up confused and with no memory of what has happened;

5) have him suddenly notice some blood smeared on his hands and clothing;

6) show a long sequence from Norman's P.O.V., as he races down to Marion's motel room and enters the bathroom to find:

7) a shot of Marion's bloody and completely dismembered body, lying like a confused jigsaw puzzle on the floor.

(After which Norman would then have *two* angry men after him for revenge: Marion's boyfriend and his homicidal step-father.)

Unfortunately, *Bates Motel* doesn't seem interested in pure horror this season—at least so far. For four long years I have been hoping, and hating, to see Norman go over the precipice into total madness—over to the dark side. As Norman himself has said, there is a "darkness" inside Mother—a cold and insane evil, frighteningly like the demon-possession depicted in *The Exorcist*. Very few people have seen this evil directly, since it rarely reveals itself, save when Norman is alone. And those who *have* been unlucky enough to see Mother rise to the surface of Norman's mind rarely survive for very long.

Bates Motel started out splendidly—but I'm worried that it might not stick the landing. Originally it was a show that had the courage of its convictions (classical storytelling, traditional values, deep characterizations), but now it appears to be sputtering out in ill-judged revisionism. What had started out as a myth is instead becoming just another "dark secrets" show, like *Breaking Bad, Nurse Jackie,* or *Weeds*.

Indeed, the premise of *Bates Motel* was probably originally sold to its network, A&E, as a mixture of *Dexter* (the serial killer motif), *Breaking Bad* (the drug-culture background), and *Twin Peaks* (atmospheric mood of menace and weirdness). But in sum total, what resulted was somehow much more than that. What redeemed *Bates Motel* from this sordid background of cable television anti-heroes and criminals was its mythic basis. Like the Greek audiences of long ago, we all knew that Norma Bates would die and that Norman would go mad. Seeing the slow progress of the gods' revenge was what made the show so compelling, and so heartbreaking. But now I'm finding some of the *changes* made to the myth even more troubling than the horrors themselves.

But it could be worse. For example, the changes made in *Bates Motel* are nothing compared to what *Psycho*'s creator, Robert Bloch, did to his own novel.

At first glance, one is tempted to read *Psycho II* (1982) as an act of rage directed against a Hollywood studio that would produce a *Psycho* sequel (*Psycho II* [1983]) without compensation or consent. The exact opposite, however, is true: Bloch began work on this novel at the instigation of his publisher, in return for an enormous stipend—and Universal Studios' *Psycho II* was only produced afterwards, in direct response to Bloch's book. Indeed, according to Bloch, Universal was quite displeased with the plot of Bloch's novel (and understandably so) and offered him the chance to novelize the film scenario instead—but Bloch refused. As Bloch observes, "I met this proposition with a straight face, but upon informing the studio what I'd received as an advance for my own novel there was nothing further except shocked silence on their part."

Apparently intending his sequel as a commentary on contemporary standards of morality and violence (or the lack thereof), Bloch (SPOILER ALERT) kills off Norman Bates in the opening chapters of his novel—Bates suddenly murdered by a transient hitchhiker whom he picks up after his own equally murderous escape from the insane asylum.

Bloch then continues his novel with a dark attack on the movie industry itself, with its fascination with shower-scenes and bloody violence. Forgetting—or perhaps regretting—that it was he himself who helped to bring these scenes to the forefront of the American consciousness, Bloch shows us perverted movie producers who enjoy dark acts of sadism and violence. The outside world, Bloch seems to be saying, is more insane than Norman Bates ever was. And if Hitchcock was able to startle 1960s audiences by abruptly killing off the heroine halfway into the film, then I'll startle them even more by abruptly killing off Norman Bates himself in the same way!

Unfortunately, it makes for a very sparse and static novel, which never really recovers from the sudden disappearance of its tragic main character. Despite the fame and notoriety that Norman Bates undoubtedly brought him, Bloch seems to have regarded his creation rather poorly.

Bloch himself seems to make an appearance in this novel, in the form of Tom Post, an elderly Hollywood screenwriter turned hotel proprietor, whose Dawn Motel in Los Angeles is a spitting image for the original Bates Motel. And one rather thinks that we hear Bloch speaking when he voices Post's derogatory view of 1980s Hollywood films:

> "Waste of time. I don't understand movies nowadays. All those sex scenes—people in bed rolling over and over. Try doing it that way and you'll end up with a broken back. And then, when he's finished, the stud pops out from under the covers and damned if he isn't wearing boxer shorts. That sure as hell isn't the way we did it in my day. . .
>
> "[. . .] Of course, times change. Take censorship. Maybe four-letter words are in, but other words are out. You don't believe me,

try getting up in public and singing the second line of 'My Old Kentucky Home.'

"[. . .] Junk food, junk films. Writers have too much power nowadays.

"[. . .] I don't mean pictures. But think about this. Some politician gets up and reads a speech. His opponent reads a rebuttal. Then a TV commentator reads a report explaining what the two men read. All of it—the speech, the rebuttal, the explanation—is the work of some anonymous writers in the back room. And we call it 'news.'"

Bloch concludes his novel (SPOILER ALERT) with his protagonist, Dr. Claiborne, going mad after he learns of the death of Norman Bates. In a clever twist, it turns out that Claiborne has been committing all the murders. As the psychiatrist explains at the end, "You couldn't let Norman die, so you became him."

Bloch continued in this satirical vein in yet another sequel, *Psycho House* (1990), in which the Bates Motel and a nearby house are resurrected as a theme park intended to capitalize and profit from the notoriety of Bates's crimes. Bloch was perhaps inspired by actual *Psycho* theme parks created by Universal Studios—but he could just as easily have been satirizing the way in which his own *Psycho* (1959) capitalized upon the heinous crimes of Ed Gein.

As the new *Bates Motel* proves, Bloch created a myth that survives—even surviving the contempt of its own creator. It survives because the United States has taken this myth to heart and recognized something of itself in it. Like Claiborne, we could not let Norman Bates die—even at the cost of going a little bit mad ourselves.

Terror for Children

Taij Devon

ARIC CUSHING. *Vampire Boy*. [N.p.]: Grand & Archer, 2016. 218 pp. ISBN: 978-1-929730-04-9: $17.99 hc. ISBN: 978-1-929730-01-8: $8.99 tpb.

Aric Cushing's children's novel *Vampire Boy* creates the atmosphere of wonder a child feels on Halloween using the tropes of old-time horror movies and J. K. Rowling's Harry Potter series. Like the

Harry Potter novels, *Vampire Boy* is a school story about a boy who faces the unknown and makes friends after his family sends him away to an ancient academy where young vampires, gargoyles, and fairies are taught how to use their supernatural abilities while not alerting humans to their existence. While *Vampire Boy* succeeds in recreating this sense of wonder for its young readers, it does not as effectively reach out to adult readers as J. K. Rowling did.

Vampire Boy opens with an appearance by Deleter, who is essentially the Voldemort of Cushing's fictional universe. Deleter's appearance is probably the most exciting part of the book because the threat of violence is palpable in these scenes. Also of interest is that Deleter is a steampunk vampire with a metal mechanism covering much of his terrible face. Such new genre mashups often result in great imaginative fun (Clay and Susan Griffith, for example). But that interest is sadly not realized, as few details of what it means are provided. One hopes those will be provided in later books.

This is where any scary phenomena end. Our hero Alex has loving parents, in a nice twist, and makes his goodbyes for boarding school. On the obligatory magical journey to school, there are a few miraculous events, including an homage to the Arthurian lady in the lake, but no real sense of danger. Upon arrival, much time is spent on the minutiae of settling into school. Naturally, it is separated into wings, which mimic the houses of a certain other supernatural boarding school. Also the topography has some Escher-like qualities and hints of mysterious goings-on. For young readers who have been, or will be, anxious about going to a new school, Alex's learning about his new environment serves as dramatic tension. But for anyone who has been faced with writing a thesis or taking quantum mechanics, Alex's adventure of buying textbooks fails even to budge the pulse rate. Some time is spent meeting new characters, some in Alex's new gang, and one notably not. Grimensa declares Alex her enemy for no discernible reason other than she is a "Mean Girl," or a "Heather" from an older movie. A series of microdramas ensue, comprised of small humiliations, working out the pecking order of the gang and establishing relationships. Again we have passages that might be dramatic to young readers, but anyone who has ever been unemployed facing a stack of bills cannot muster any more enthusiasm than a gentle smile.

At this point a plot arrives to save the novel from being nothing more than a day in the life. The students are presented with a riddle from the headmaster on the night before classes begin, one that is supposed to have a terribly important but undisclosed prize for whoever solves it. Competing gangs of students set off on something similar to a scavenger hunt or geolocation game, hunting for clues in their attempts to solve the mystery. In a break from the usual form of the school story, Alex is not really the leader in his gang. Events ensue that the characters find slightly ominous, or at least exciting, but all prove to be less dangerous than my habit of tree climbing when I was eight. Cushing does a disservice to the prodigious imaginative effort of his work by constantly reassuring the reader that everything will be okay, although this type of reassurance in the face of danger is a typical characteristic of novels written for children.

A bright spot in this latter section of the book is the pugenstein, a creature less funny than "Scraps" the dog sewn together by Igor in Terry Pratchett's Discworld series, but even more adorable. The pugenstein is, as its name suggests, a pug dog with bolts on its head similar to those on the head of Frankenstein's creature as represented in James Whale's 1931 film. The pugenstein is one of those "threats" that turn out to be benign; it is some sort of guard dog. *Vampire Boy* goes so far as to have parents show up at the end worried, who then are reassured, along with the reader, that there was never any danger. For a young Harry Potter fan, *Vampire Boy* may be a perfect gift. For adults, it is best employed as a read-aloud "scary" story that will not give their children nightmares.

The Homely Commonplace and the Unimaginably Deranged: J. G. Ballard's *High Rise*

Alexander Lugo

Now trite, Lovecraft's famous assertion that "The oldest and strongest emotion of mankind is fear, and the oldest and strongest kind of fear is fear of the unknown" nevertheless remains axiomatic for weird fiction. Since Lovecraft has become so inexorably embedded in the collective consciousness of our popular culture, the basic tenets of his fiction no longer appear in any way, shape, or form delimited by the oft rigid and arbitrary principles of the exclusively "weird." Retroactively, then, Lovecraft's fundamental insight into the nature of horror and why we read it, into the curious, quasi-masochistic thrill of exploring the depths of that most fearful entity, which we do not and likely cannot comprehend, may be applied both low and high: Judge Holden cast as Nyarlathotep, the indeterminate chaos of *Gravity's Rainbow* as Azathoth.

Indeed, Lovecraft's horror of the unknown is so flexible an aesthetic because it trades not in the diacritically pigeonholing elements that taint so much genre fiction; nary a ghost, vampire, or werewolf in sight (at least, not in the traditional sense of these terms). His horrors pack their punch because they are believable, in that they are part and parcel of the very fabric of the universe we know and inhabit, and so too are they, therefore, *close:* Lovecraftian revelations reek of proximity, their ghoulish truths blooming forth from beneath the otherwise blasé veneer of spring flowers and churchyards. Lovecraftian horror is eminently supernormal, and in that respect so many writers, from Jack London to Cormac McCarthy, may be said to exchange in its uncanny attributes.

J. G. Ballard, neither highbrow enough to be labeled yet another boring postmodernist nor lowbrow enough to be lost to the pulps, is a fine example of a literary, yet "weird," writer in his own right; a cartographer of the involutions of a gargantuan media landscape long before its ostensible birth in our present age, and a prescient prescriber of the accelerated pathologies and horrors that accompany its development. In his classic novel *High Rise,* first published in 1975, Ballard explores the horror of the unknown apropos the ineffable and unhallowed depths of mankind itself, simultaneously exposing the superficially quotidian social and technological developments of the luxury apartment, a metaphorical social computer of sorts arranging its denizens like self-sufficient data in a gelid server, as a vehicle for its subjects to engage with pent-up, primeval drives. In the process, the lines between building and bodies blur, engendering a moral vacuum that accommodates, like the accoutrements of the building's luxurious facilities, all the needs for a repressed mob of bored capitalists to express their most barbaric drives and desires. The building's inhabitants wander fatally through the occulted nightmare gulfs of their own selves, providing the reader with a sense of dreadful expectancy not unlike that which Lovecraft evokes with his obscure, barbarous cosmos or Ligotti with his vivid portrayals of a fraudulent consciousness.

All these writers trade in turning our knowns into unknowns, in distorting the appearance and content of the normal into the uncannily supernormal. In *High Rise,* Ballard begins with such a reconfiguration of normalcy's definition: an *in medias res* cut to one of the novel's principal characters, Dr. Robert Laing, sitting "on his balcony eating the dog." Ballard's novel moves in inconspicuously flexing gradients toward barbarity, seamlessly oscillating between the homely commonplace and the unimaginably deranged. One receives this impression from the aforementioned jump forward in the plot, during which Laing, months into the social and moral degradation of his apartment building, notes how the building's fashionable "forty floors and thousand apartments, its supermarket and swimming pools, bank and junior school . . . offered more than enough opportunities for violence and confrontation." Less a critique of consumerism, Ballard feeds its archetypes into a psychomotor dynamo, fueling a portrayal of the moral void beyond the accelerationist doom of the culture he critiques, its savage future emanating from its own elements.

The sickly ease with which Ballard's prose dips into and out of the macabre mirrors the unaccountably swift facility with which his characters turn into monsters, their space haunted. Much like Lovecraft's distortions of time, space, and our knowledge thereto, Ballard expertly suspends the oft-unquestioned cohesion of a logical universe, a situation Laing muses upon with cool aloofness: "he was surprised that there had been no obvious beginning, no point beyond which their lives had moved into a clearly more sinister dimension."

The uncanny and undefined rests brooding over the surface of this (once) normal circumstance, this slice of late twentieth-century bourgeois life, like the rectilinear, priapismic sprawl of its high-rise's forty floors. Though the novel quickly shifts back in time, before its breakdown of all moral and social conventions, this glimpse at nomadic, dog-eating barbarity presses upon everything like pentimento, slowly cracking through the chalky frame of the everyday in vibrant carmine.

Ballard's depiction of "normal" is never normal, the everyday but a face below which teem terrors grafted into our civilized behaviors. The technology of the high-rise, a self-sufficient vertical city isolated from the world, allows its natives to pierce together in the seclusion of their prison-like confines the dissociated facts, situations, schemes, ideologies, drives, and desires mutated deep within their unconscious lives, ushering forth nightmares that always were and will be, however mysterious and unknowable they may and likely will remain. Ballard's human is a transdimensional monstrosity unto itself.

This notion of a subject increasingly aware of its dual life, conscious and unconscious, civilized and animalistic, is doubled again by the very nature of the high-rise, bought and built for "peace, quiet and anonymity," yet, as mentioned earlier, made also to offer infinite situations for its inhabitants to cannibalize one another. Ballard plays with these strange paradoxes gleefully, often linking the contradictions of the building's structure with parallel contradictions within its inhabitants' collective psyche: "[Laing] now squatted beside a fire of telephone directories, eating the roast hindquarter of the Alsatian before setting off to his lecture at the medical school." The comfort of the high-rise's sedate realm, in which all is, at first, known and unquestioned, stages its own mutation as the unknown dimensions of the human heart burst through the insidious cracks of a superficial micro-civilization, concomitantly reconfiguring the function of the building itself. Its meaning and contents become but a projection of the habits and ideas of its subjects. With the protean grace of a phantasmagoric fever-dream, an apartment building becomes a totem for a moral, social, and subjective space of utmost novelty, one so ineffably fantastic as to be conceived only as a supreme, domineering absolute, as tenaciously inextricable as time itself, operating by way of the alien semiotics of a future beyond the negotiable symbols of capitalist culture; in short, a violent, carnivorous sublimity.

Under Ballard's sweeping suspension of normal laws, the horrors of the unknown introduce more than a fickle dichotomy between civilized and savage behaviors among which the latter gradually emerges out from the veneer of the former. For when Laing, alarmed by the sudden impact of a wine bottle upon his balcony floor, jettisoned out from a party located among the upper, increasingly elitist floors, coldly considers how the lack of concern "about the ultimate destination of this missile" correlates with the tendency for the building's residents "not to care about tenants more than two floors below them," we are likely reminded of our own casual apathy in regard to the lives of our more "distant" neighbors, however harmless this may seem. For Ballard, even these instances of normative callousness are symptomatic of an incomprehensible pathology endemic to civilized life; in this case, the arbitrary distance imposed between that which we should and should not care about.

As the high-rise's isolated inhabitants drift closer together and splinter back into marauding tribes in a rhythmic back-and-forth, Ballard surveys the unquestioned absence of empathy and connection in daily life. In doing so, he exposes how seemingly subterranean horrors lurking beneath the surface of the everyday stem from and indeed constitute it. Further complicating the novel's mess of paradoxes, we find here a strange friction between a competitive society of isolated individuals and the fractured sense of community afforded by the "virtually homogeneous collection of well-to-do professional people" living within "a huge machine designed to serve, not the collective body of tenants, but the individual resident in isolation." This "perfect background into which Laing could merge invisibly" is constantly threatened by the sense of isolated community to which the high-rise gives shape. The friction therein is clearly present from the raucous party Laing takes note of in the novel's first pages—a growing partnership of callous beings.

This dialectical friction between a competitive society of individuals, self-imposing an upward-moving caste system based on floor level of residence, who have an innate need for community is made problematic, to say the least, by a social structure in which members of a common, "homogeneous" class are treated, at first, as members of different species. The invisibility herein renders the subjectivity of a cutthroat capitalist schema void, to which selves become lost in a nexus of other selves, forming the groundwork of a suicidal partnership society, like a Çatalhöyük of murderous schizophrenics. The tension established, the quantum troubling of a subjectivity lost between its singularized measure within a rigid, individualized compartmentalization and its wash in a multiplicitously measured communal swarm, springboards the high-rise's denizens into hyperpathology; a Frankensteinian collective creature assembled of questionable, modern norms and repressed, unconscious urges. Ballard, channeling a Lovecraftian dread of the unknown, may leave us viewing our Facebook and Twitter friends and followers through a more kaleidoscopic, vicious lens, beyond which a new configuration of subjectivity awaits, savage and cruel to our "civilized," and thereby epistemologically limited, eyes.

The high-rise's inhabitants, in this process of existential metamorphosis, cast all moral, social, and behavioral conventions in a blinding, alien light. Characters quickly become sensitive to the paradoxical feelings that their isolated community provokes, to the alien feelings with which their civilized behaviors have no symbolic order to express without contradiction. Thus, Laing, though he "had come to the high-rise to get away from all relationships," continues to fixate upon the high-rise's abundant potential for romantic flings, the proximity of intrigued women noted by Laing "with a fascinated but cautious eye." And so Laing "found himself becoming more romantic and more callous at the same time." Moral horror becomes a concern of language, the extent to which it may simultaneously be capable of expressing the desires of a human animal while doing so in a way sensible to social convention, an impossibility the novel quickly presents as such. Laing is caught craving sympathy, communion, love, these basic human attributes he simultaneously feels and desires to be alienated from. Despite the congestion, however isolated individually, of the building's residents, the chances for intimacy it establishes seem poorly negotiable by the methods of conventional social and moral language. Laing is unable to love in any way he currently knows, but, like everyone else in the building, the isolation, self-sufficiency, and repression of the spaces within which he and the rest of the residents are sorted quickly begin to give shape to an equally internal and external world of its own, part of and detached from the building and inhabitants, one that trades in the complete lack of restrictions and thereby offers simultaneously a chance for humanity to reconfigure itself with new values more appropriate perhaps than those derived from the language of a "sane" world, and the danger-fraught abandon of a moral vacuum. That this troubling exists between moral vacuum and partnership society is telling. Human communication, so far as we may gauge it through Ballard's contradictory micro-civilization, appears intrinsically pathological.

As such, normalcy cannot normalize anything, and deviant perversity is, at best, a failed expression of that which conventional behavior also fails to accommodate. The strange and the commonplace, the lecherous and the romantic, the callous and the violent all appear equally savage and without border. This indeterminacy is belied by the sheer geography of the novel's terrain: "The massive scale of the glass and concrete architecture, and its striking situation on a bend of the river, sharply separated the development project from the rundown areas around it, decaying nineteenth-century terraced houses and empty factories already zoned for reclamation." Of course, the sense of surrounding decay offset by the high-rise's superficial status as an insular liberal paradise is a deliberately weak decoy; the hideous, ravenous underbelly of human consciousness and behavior cannot be separated by anything so stark, so obvious. Just as, for Lovecraft, science threatened mankind with a premature acknowledgment of its own infelicitously doomed position in the cosmos, so for Ballard does the seeming progressions of a capitalistic, socially stratified society give way to forces that realize and empower primal, irrational, and bloodthirsty drives. The contradiction therein threatens our very conception of subjectivity.

For Ballard, technological progression is tantamount to a hideous form of accelerationism, tainted not with a dubious political eschatology, but with the chillingly reasonable conception of a reborn moral wasteland akin only to prehistorical animosity, a holocaust of ecstasy and freedom that evolution sought to cancel and preserve like waxen statues of a dead past, dead but dreaming. As Laing recalls, "Six months earlier, when he had sold the lease of his Chelsea house and moved to the security of the high-rise, he had travelled forward fifty years in time." What he does not yet know is what waits in the horizon: a space within which enters a "new world" of discombobulated mores and symbols, where "the large dog on the spit resembled the flying figure of a mutilated man, soaring with immense energy across the night sky, embers glowing with the fire of jewels in his skin."

Still, traces of "civilized" behavior emerge within the novel's paradoxical order, most conspicuously in the form of social demarcations. Yet from their first appearance, Laing, like many other anarchistic inhabitants, notes the utterly "facile" element whereby people are socially identified "by the floors on which they lived." In the socio-moral isolation of the high-rise, the absurdity of such proprietary nonsense is flushed vulgar, yet in the drift toward a clean slate, a self-sufficient techno-historic organism, utopia does not await. Again we return to the novel's ghoulish, extra-linguistic event-horizon, for beyond the flimsy demarcations of a micro-civilization awaits only the horror of the void that remains in the wake of shattered symbols, a void within which resides our unconscious selves made conscious in alien displacement. As one character, Helen Wilder, puts it, in response to her awareness of incipient hostilities, "It's almost as if these aren't the people who really live here." As the novel briskly progresses across its slim, 200-page span, characters shift without pause from elements of the human homogeneous elite to "secret agents unconvincingly trying to establish a . . . role," and then to beasts that evolve into something truly novel, unaccountable yet undeniably real, supranormal yet crude, absurd yet dense with biological sensibility. To call this movement uncanny would be a gross understatement.

In the closing chapter of *High-Rise,* Richard Wilder, a director of documentaries, tries to speak to a semi-nude, knife-wielding young woman while chewing on a roasted cat, "but found himself grunting, unable to form the words with his broken teeth and scarred tongue." Ascending the floors to the top, he carries a camera with him, originally intending to shoot a film concerning the psychological and social vexations of high-rise life. By the time he reaches the top, camera still in hand, "he was no longer certain what its function was, or why he had kept it with him for so long." Upon seeing his wife on the roof, named Helen, the narrator reports that "Despite her change of dress he recognized her as his wife Judith." Horror works at its best, particularly of the weird and cosmic brand, when its revelations, its excursions into the unknown and forbidden render that which before was drab and familiar utterly alien. In the best of Lovecraft's work, all terrestrial history, from its genesis onwards, is cast in the inconceivable light of the findings of scholarly recluses and Antarctic expeditioners. In Ligotti's, human consciousness, the mode through which we "know" ourselves and our world, remains, in the wake of revelation, nothing more a trick of processes, a puppet-master to no good end. From a socio-behavioral perspective, Ballard does something similar with *High-Rise,* exposing a micro-civilization or vertical city suspended in a tug-and-pull between isolated community and technological advancement, harboring the latent savagery of mankind in such a way as to enable it to burst on a scale of condensed isolation and unaccountability, a neo-history of the world launched forth into a retrogression of its values, the latter rendered specious by the exorbitant self-consciousness of its trapped yet free denizens. Every act, gesture, and slip, from their inconspicuous beginnings onward, is fraught with dread, with the horrific potency of a trigger, a bomb, a gnashing of ravenous, rapacious teeth. What is left behind is largely unnamable. With great and terrible foresight, Ballard maps a territory mankind currently explores, namely by way of social media, a landscape to itself, out of which, as technology individualizes and connects us more and more, a new form of subjectivity gestates, and therefore a new bogeyman, beyond all good and evil, beyond expression and accommodation, a veritable unknown horror whose outline is given shape in this wonderfully weird novel.

The Resurgence of Weird Magazines

Ashley Dioses

In the past couple of years there has been a resurgence of independent journals and magazines that cater to the weird, horror, and fantasy genres. With the help from social media, the weird has emerged from the shadows and has made itself known in many groups and circles that might have passed it unnoticed. Pop culture has also helped shed light on their original foundations and roots with comic-based movies and conventions. I am proud to say that I have been in a few of these publications. As I am a relatively new writer on the scene, these publications have provided great opportunities for me to get my work out there, while also allowing me to read a wide assortment of offerings from other new and established genre writers.

Xnoybis by Dunhams Manor Press holds a special place in my heart. It was the first publication to pay me a professional rate for my work. I was just starting out in 2014 and I don't believe I was published in anything much, except for *Spectral Realms* No. 1 by Hippocampus Press, so when I received my acceptance email, I was blown away. I was getting $25 for a poem; five times the professional rate, according to the Horror Writers Association, for poetry! *Xnoybis,* edited by Jordan Krall, was released in June 2015 and is a quarterly journal of weird fiction, which also contains poetry, articles, and interviews. The third issue of *Xnoybis* will also be the first themed issue, with a focus on Pan. Issue 4's theme will be "Rumours of Leviathan: Conspiratorial Weird Fiction," and issue 5's theme will be a tribute to Fritz Leiber's *Our Lady of Darkness*. Scheduled for later this year, issue 3 will feature stories by DJ Tyrer, C. M. Muller, Matt Leyshon, and Jonas Moth and poetry by Adam Bolivar and myself.

Weirdbook Magazine was relaunched in September 2015 with W. Paul Ganley's blessing and continued with issue 31 after the original run ended in 1997. It is now published by Wildside Press and run by senior editor and publisher David A. Riley and managing editor and fiction editor Douglas Draa. Its goal is to follow closely the atmosphere of sword-and-sorcery and weird fiction as the original run did. *Weirdbook* is now on issue 34, with its first themed anthology in the works, which looks to be an annual publication. The issue will be composed of original fiction and poetry. Since issue 31, *Weirdbook* has featured writers such as John R. Fultz, Adrian Cole, Gary A. Braunbeck, Darrell Schweitzer, Jessica Amanda Salmonson, Leeman Kessler, Scott R Jones, C. M. Muller, Franklyn Searight, Frederick J. Mayer, Wade German, Chad Hensley, K. A. Opperman, myself, to name but a few.

Skelos: The Journal of Weird Fiction and Dark Fantasy, by Skelos Press, is run by Mark Finn, Chris Gruber, and Jeffrey Shanks. Shanks contacted me and invited me to submit to this new, pulpy weird journal. I have, so far, not been disappointed in submitting to any of these new weird periodicals, so I wasn't about to stop. I was more than happy to dig up some poems and submit them. *Skelos* is jam-packed with fiction, poetry, articles, essays, reviews, and art with a sword-and-sorcery and Robert E. Howard bent. Writers such as Keith Taylor, Scott A. Cupp, Dave Hardy, Frank Coffman, Pat Calhoun, Bobby Derie, W. H. Pugmire, Cynthia Ward, Robert M. Price, K. A. Opperman, myself, and many others grace these pages. *Skelos* has just released their second issue.

I first heard of *The Audient Void: A Journal of Weird Fiction and Dark Fantasy* through a fellow poet who met the editor, Obadiah Baird, at a party. The title itself already struck me as something I'd be interested in, and I immediately inquired more about it. It is a weird and dark fantasy periodical that publishes fiction, poetry, and nonfiction. The first issue, now sold out, was released in June 2016 and contained stories from David Barker, Daniel Pietersen, and Sarah Walker, and poetry by W. H. Pugmire, Wade German, Dan Clore, Adam Bolivar, K. A. Opperman, and myself. The cover art was done by Allen Koszowski with interior illustrations done by him and Sarah Walker. *The Audient Void* has just released its third issue.

I arrived to the party late with *Ravenwood Quarterly,* as I did with *Xnoybis,* and didn't know it existed until the submissions call for issue 2. Edited by Travis Neisler, *Ravenwood* debuted in August 2016. Whereas other weird journals seem to focus on fantasy, *Ravenwood* seeks to publish darker and weirder fiction, poetry, and art. *Ravenwood* has structured each issue around a theme. These include Halloween/autumn, noir, goat, Halloween/autumn again, yellow/Decadent, and Swamp Occult. They are currently on issue 3, with release dates for the upcoming issues forthcoming. Contributing writers have included Donald Armfield, Philip Fracassi, Scott Thomas, Brian O'Connell, S. L. Edwards, Russell Smeaton, Matthew M. Bartlett, Peter Rawlik, Sam Gafford, Christopher Ropes, Joseph Bouthiette Jr., Michael Faun, Jordan Krall, K. A. Opperman, myself, and others.

The next two publications are international zines, hailing from France and Sweden respectively. The first is *Nightgaunt* by Cephaloprod, run by Adam Joffrain, which was released in April 2015. *Nightgaunt* is a lovely French fanzine with the stated purpose of bringing awareness to the weird from the French- and English-speaking worlds. Each zine contains English and French writers with a translation of each piece, be it prose or poetry. It was awesome seeing a poem of mine translated into French in issue 3. *Nightgaunt* is currently working on its fifth issue and has had writers such as W. H. Pugmire, Ran Cartwright, Chrystel Duchamp, Chad Hensley, Leigh Blackmore, and Frédéric Gaillard within its pages.

Feverish Fiction Magazine, by Sleazy Viking Press, is edited by Michael Faun and caters to fans of "pulpy, sleazy flash stories and poetry." Its first issue came out in December 2016 and it has roughly come out with an issue per month—no small feat! Writers include Justin A. Mank, Patrick Winters, Konstantine Paradias, Paul Boswell, Nycole Laff, S. C. Burke, Lee Clark Zumpe, Donald Armfield, K. A. Opperman, myself, and others. For diehard sleaze fans who desire more, Sleazy Viking Press has recently come out with *Feverish Fiction Magazine*'s sister zine, *Feverish Chixxx,* also edited by Michael Faun, which contains occult themed pieces and nude occult photography.

These next four publications I quickly procured when I discovered them. *Nightscript,* edited by C. M. Muller, was first released in October 2015 and comes out annually with strange tales of the supernatural and weird. *Cirsova,* edited by P. Alexander, is a magazine heavily focused on science fiction and sword-and-planet. It first came out in spring 2016. *Turn to Ash,* edited by Benjamin Holesapple, is a "print-only horror fiction zine." They are, however, currently seeking a poetry editor to add to the team. The first issue came out in August 2016. And the newest to the weird bunch is *Occult Detective Quarterly,* run by John Linwood Grant, Sam Gafford, and Travis Neisler, which came out in January of this year. *Occult Detective Quarterly* publishes fiction, nonfiction, and art (including a comic strip, "Borkchito: Occult Doggo Detective," by Sam L. Edwards and Yves Tourigny) relating to investigating the supernatural and occult of various eras.

Fans of the weird have reason to rejoice again as these new magazines continue to produce new stories and reveal fresh takes on the genre. New and established voices now have more venues to showcase their hard-to-place work and niche pieces.

The Final Work of Mark Fisher

James Machin

MARK FISHER. *The Weird and the Eerie.* London: Repeater, 2017. 144 pp. ISBN: 978-1-910924-38-9. $14.95 tpb.

The 11 March 2017 edition of the *Los Angeles Review of Books* included a lengthy "In Memoriam" piece, rounding up testimonies of former colleagues and friends regarding the late writer Mark Fisher. That his loss was and is an exorbitant one is abundantly evident from the outpouring of grief, bewilderment, and affirmations of Fisher's brilliance contained therein.

An academic and writer whose work appeared in *Sight & Sound,* the *Wire,* and the *Guardian,* his *Capitalist Realism* (Zer0 Books, 2009) has a growing reputation as one of the definitive responses to the international banking crisis of 2008. Fisher's interest in genre was never separated from his wider cultural criticism, and his work was replete with references to cult 1970s horror television and film, hauntology, science fiction (Tarkovsky was a regular touchstone), and the weird. As he says in his introduction to the volume: "I have been fascinated and haunted by examples of the weird and the eerie for as long as I can remember."

Indeed, it was Fisher who convened the conferences discussing Lovecraft and critical theory in 2007 at Goldsmiths University in London, which did a good deal to catalyse the twenty-first-century appropriation of Lovecraft by philosophers and theorists developing their thinking in such recondite areas as Object Oriented Ontology. Despite the ease with which he engaged with such esoteric discourses, Fisher's prose is—mercifully for the reader—always lucid and elegant. This leaves him happily accessible to those who have no stomach for the tortuous opacity and prolixity of many of those who dream in the witch house of contemporary cultural studies.

The clarity of Fisher's thinking and his expression of that thinking are never more evident than in *The Weird and the Eerie*. Fisher's central thesis can be boiled down to the simple assertion that "the weird" represents a *presence* ("of that which does not belong") while "the eerie" represents an *absence* (of that which we would expect to be present, normally some type of human agency). Working from this cogent basis, Fisher conducts a survey of a range of texts, music, and films, to elaborate upon how these two notions find expression through them—and how further meaning can be gleaned from examining them in these contexts.

Fisher is careful to differentiate both the weird and the eerie from the horrific: "What the weird and the eerie have in common is a preoccupation with the strange. The strange—not the horrific." This is only the first of many echoes of Lovecraft's own theorizing on similar matters; the notion that the weird has to have something rather more than "sheets and bloody bones" in order to count as such. And like Lovecraft, the weird and the eerie are, for Fisher, registers or modes rather than genres. Fisher points out that they are to be found "at the edges of genres such as horror and science fiction," but that these "genre associations have obscured what is specific to the weird and the eerie." (Again, commensurate with Lovecraft's assertion that the weird mode is identifiable in texts that cannot identified as weird in and of themselves.)

It is naturally to Lovecraft that Fisher turns to begin his survey in the first section of the book on "The Weird." The obtrusion of the weird into the quotidian not only disturbs through simple category pollution—just think of all those Lovecraftian hybrids: human and animal; different categories of animal; the animal and the monstrous; the mineral and the biological; and myriad combinations thereof. On a profounder level than these monstrous hybrids is the "egress" of another, non-anthropocentric, world into our own, and it is this which creates the payload of so many of Lovecraft's stories: "the problem of worlds—of contact between incommensurable worlds." Fisher hits the nail firmly on the head with his defense of Lovecraft against the charge of poor or absent characterization in his narratives: "Lovecraft needs the human world, for much the same reason that a painter of a vast edifice might insert a standard human figure standing before it: to provide a sense of scale." Such sentences bring their own weird, disconcerting charge to Fisher's nonfictional writing.

Using Lovecraft as a springboard, Fisher goes on to examine a variety of material, from H. G. Wells to the sardonic postpunk of Manchester band The Fall, David Lynch's films to the narco-paranoia of Philip K. Dick's unique iterations of science fiction. In all these, Fisher demonstrates the weird's propensity to disorient and destabilise, to "create a weird architecture, in which no interior space is ever secure for long, and gateways to the outside can open up practically anywhere." Indeed, the range and variety of material discussed by Fisher perhaps serve as a double-edged sword. Although Lovecraft is central to Fisher's thesis, and M. R. James makes several appearances, *The Weird and the Eerie* is notable for the absence of many of the obvious names associated with canonical weird fiction. While this may be disappointing or baffling for some readers, in actual fact it serves to abstract the essence of the mode: the book's work of identifying the register in such a diverse range of cultural manifestations arguably reveals far more about the weird and the eerie than might a simple run-through of the usual suspects. Fisher uses the paradigms he establishes to pull focus on texts in revelatory ways, a wonderful example of this being his take on Margaret Atwood's early novel *Surfacing*. Indeed, Fisher's discussion of the eerie in *Surfacing*, juxtaposing it with Jonathan Glazer's 2013 film *Under the Skin*, immediately suggests (to this reader) its consideration as a resonant antecedent to Jeff VanderMeer's recent Southern Reach trilogy.

It is certainly difficult to imagine that a book that draws lines between the folk song "Tam Lin," Nigel Kneale's *Quatermass,* and

Alan Garner could ever be a dull read. Still, eyebrows may be raised over whether or not, for example, Fassbinder's presence is perhaps too strained a contrivance (as insightful as Fisher's critique of Fassbinder's 1973 film *Welt am Draht* is). However, more often than not, Fisher sets out his case convincingly and satisfyingly: although I am far less forgiving of the glops of schmaltz splattered throughout Christopher Nolan's *Interstellar* (2016), Fisher does a fine job of demonstrating the eerie through discussion of the absences and bleak exteriority writ large in the cosmos; of an "aoenic" sense of time, of endless "chains of influence and causation" that he also identifies in Kubrick's *2001* and *The Shining* and Tarkovsky's *Stalker*.

This cosmicism of course brings us back full circle to Lovecraft, and Fisher's decision not to attempt to surgically differentiate the weird and the eerie is a wise one. His closing discussion of *Picnic at Hanging Rock* (both the 1975 film and the 1967 novel on which it was based) concludes that it "occupies some space between" the modes; most of the texts he discusses, whether filmic or literary, could no doubt be convincingly argued to do the same.

As a work of criticism *The Weird and the Eerie* is a lucid and eminently coherent thesis. At numerous points in the book, Fisher presents a crucial insight with stunning economy (just a single example being: "Behind all of the manifestations of the eerie, the central enigma at its core is the problem of agency"). This review only hints at some of the myriad points of intellectual departure that *The Weird and the Eerie* provokes in the reader; provocations and intimations that suggest re-readings will be both necessary and productive. In this, as well as his stylistic restraint, Fisher reminds one of John Gray, the philosopher and critic who has also discussed the weird and the eerie in the *New Statesman* and for the BBC. Like Gray's best work, *The Weird and the Eerie* achieves that rare feat of being a nonfiction page-turner. Fisher's choices may puzzle the dedicated niche consumer of the weird (not forgetting the eerie), but even if one's tastes are far from catholic, anyone with an interest in genre writing will be endlessly entertained and enlightened by Fisher's book. It is a painfully sad thing that it will be his last.

SMASH EVERYTHING!
Bobby Rhodes and His *Demons*

Nathan Chazan

> He wanted to talk about the strange passion that catches hold of a man by the scruff of his neck and transports him to a realm beyond the fear of death.—Yukio Mishima, *The Sailor Who Fell from Grace with the Sea*

A black pimp named Tony walks into a movie theater. He's coarse and crude and his girls love him. Moreover, he is noisy—dubbed over somewhat questionably in English with an Oscar the Grouchian snarl, the pimp and his posse are a caricature of the disruption and discomfort often provoked in "polite society" by the very presence of disprivileged minorities. However, the fellow filmgoers bothered by this racially coded noise will soon lose interest in crusty class distinctions, due to a rapidly invasive zombie horde. The movie they were watching was shit anyway, but the film they are characters in—Lamberto Bava and Dario Argento's *Demons* (1985)—is one of the most wildly entertaining horror flicks of its time.

Argento had produced a number of his own films before, but *Demons* was his first production for another director. *Demons* fits neatly into a particular strain of the Argento filmography, alongside *Tenebre* (1982), *Opera* (1987), and *The Stendhal Syndrome* (1996), in which the act of viewing horror is a catalyst to violence. Argento takes the age-old panic that seeing violent media will make people violent and uses that fear as a narrative hook to explore within that very sort of deviant horror. In *The Stendhal Syndrome,* insanity is induced by the empathetic experience of art; *Opera*'s killer wishes to make the heroine a murderer through her witness to his actions; the bloodbaths of *Tenebre* are motivated by response to the text of a murder mystery. *Demons* is overtly about cinema, an evil version of Woody Allen's *The Purple Rose of Cairo* (released the same year, 1985), in which the viewing of a scary movie makes its events real as well as its consequences. It is eventually a dumb film about survival and set pieces, but the very process of becoming such makes its brilliance stronger. Trapped in the theater, becoming zombies, reality devolves into genre logic.

As the cinema descends into diabolical chaos, one man emerges prepared for the chaos: Tony the pimp, portrayed by Bobby Rhodes. He is a man who feels compassion ("Holy shit! She's a friend of mine!") and yet exercises authority with clarity and basic wisdom.

"QUIET! QUIET!" he roars. "WE NEED TO FIND THE EXIT!" When his assemblage of scared teens and film patrons find there is none, Tony gets a better idea. As the exhausted group begins to blame the movie for their woes, Tony seizes on this notion and barrels up toward the projection booth. The booth is a strange place, a futuristic and unfathomable automation. The machinery is evil and awesome, but it is also clearly fragile.

"SMASH EVERYTHING!" Tony proclaims, repeating the phrase two or three more times. Tony's immolating howl is brief but iconic, a guttural cry that becomes something of an ambient anthem in memory if not on screen. This rhythmic voice of destruction climaxes as Tony tears the film out of its reel, warping the projection to his will until the film stops for good. The actual movie then cuts to a group of punks we haven't seen before driving around Berlin while a pop song plays with lyrics that contrast "inside" and "outside." Those punks will be important to the story later, but for now this brief, jarring break from the zombie nightmare suggests a metaphysical victory for Tony the pimp: he really did stop the movie for a second there.

The revolution ends and we're back on the theater balcony. Tony orders his loyal followers to construct a barricade. While instructing one guy to use his blood-spattered knife, Tony is ambushed by several new demons and goes down swinging. What's great about his death scene is that it's not really anyone's fault; the kids are scared but not dumb, and Tony is assertive but not hubristic. The demons' consumption of Tony is at most an oversight, but plays more as inevitability. Tony never looks stronger in the film than when he is dying, his musculature amplified by the swarming monsters' grip. Tony's end is intercut with more footage of the punks from before, snorting coke strong enough to "wake up the dead." No escaping Demons.

A later iconic sequence in which a silhouetted demon horde

emerges up a flight of stairs under a pooling blue light (it's on the poster!) positions the zombified Tony as if their leader, destined to command even in the underworld.

Tony is now undead, and so too is the *Demons* franchise. The film was popular enough on VHS to spawn a whole line of films purported to be *Demons* sequels from the likes of Bava, Umberto Lenzi, Michele Soavi, and Luigi Cozzi. However, only one of these films is an actual *Demons* movie as opposed to simply bearing the brand for international video markets. That movie is *Demons 2* (1986), reuniting director Bava, producer Argento, and memorable character actor Bobby Rhodes.

Demons 2 takes the basic structure of its precursor and smashes it together with a version of J. G. Ballard's *High-Rise* devoid of sexuality and subtext, peppered with imitations of memorable bits from *The Thing, Videodrome,* and *Gremlins,* and the TV studio from Umberto Lenzi's *Nightmare City*. While *Demons 2* is less aesthetically powerful than the first while still visually potent, there is depth to be found in it—but mainly through allusion, empty signifiers to be filled out by the horror buff's memory. The main engine of the film is powered instead by the propulsive energy of genre junk at its purest.

In *Demons 2,* Rhodes's character has been upgraded to a much more legitimate profession as a fitness instructor, decked out in tight Village People clothing accentuating his bodily contours. Although this is perhaps a more ridiculous getup than his suave white pimp suit, Rhodes here is a professional, albeit one outfitted to the tune of the aerobic eighties. The fitness instructor has a name, Hank, but for the purposes of this essay, and since he is never referred to by name within the film, the character will be treated as an incarnation of Bobby Rhodes himself.

The real-life Bobby Rhodes, the actor, has had many bit parts in Italian genre films over the years, namely in the Lou Ferrigno *Hercules,* but his work on the two *Demons* movies is by far his best known and most notable. Rhodes is clearly wise to this and has produced a series of documentary videos hosted on his YouTube channel entitled "Bobby Rhodes: Through Horror and Back." These questionably informative clips focus on Rhodes sitting around on a couch and talking about how he was in the *Demons* movies. In one episode, "*Demons* and the Girls," Rhodes lists every actress who worked on the two films and compliments their personalities. Like many great footnotes in the '80s horror canon, Rhodes is trapped in the festival and convention circuit, a purgatorial space where boundless enthusiasm is married to the stifling of creativity. Yet within that boulevard of broken fandoms a legend is perpetually resurrected, the legend of Bobby Rhodes, screen icon, demon slayer.

Bobby Rhodes the character, the fitness instructor, is not the same man who first took on the demons, but his soul bears the imprint of Tony the pimp's struggles. He is a reincarnation of a fiction given new weight, hewn from the iron bars of the gymnasium. Bobby Rhodes is not going to be surprised by the demons. This is not a sequel where the phrase "Oh no, not again!" will be uttered. Whether he knows it or not, Bobby is ready, waiting to spring into action.

The core of Bobby's progression can be understood in his professional upgrade. A pimp is a marginal figure, powerful only within the confines of his extralegal territory. The fitness instructor is a designated authority with an official expectation to be strong and make others strong. The iconic pimp controls his flock through fear and psychic domination of those scared and disenfranchised with nowhere else to turn. The army of a fitness instructor has consented enthusiastically to their task of bettering themselves as individuals and as a group under the guidance of a sympathetic trainer. The Rhodites of *Demons 2* are more egalitarian, collectivized, and mobilized than their predecessors, disciplined bodies made vibrant by colorful leotards. Spartacus is back, and he's shooting zombies.

Everything happens just as before, only more terrific. The first of Bobby's clan to go are crushed by exercise machinery, their biceps made martyrs. Bobby and the gang smash their way down the lower levels of the apartment complex, finally steamrolling into the garage. When the garage doors won't open, the Rhodites diligently crash cars into this boundary, an act of appealing destruction with the promise of salvation. When a bodybuilder can't seem to hack the complexities of operating a fire extinguisher, Bobby admonishes him: "YOU'RE ALL MUSCLE AND NO BRAINS, BOY!" Bobby's followers are not meant to be mindless worker drones, but to strive for excellence and initiative even under this greatest of pressures.

A barricade is constructed, and refugees from the upper levels are admitted. Among these wretched innocents is a young Asia Argento (whose father is played by director Bava), a witness to the simulated screen violence and mayhem wreaked by the collaboration of her real and fictional fathers. The barrier to the outside world proves itself impermeable, while the demons will inevitably pass through their obstruction. The Rhodites prepare to fight what will be an absolute bloodbath, an inferno of fire and car wrecks and blood and shouting and muscles and weapons. They fail, yet the battle is beautiful. A pregnant couple separated from Bobby's army will later escape from the roof. The point of Bobby Rhodes's last stand is not victory but spectacle. The demons will not be as iconic as his resistance.

Bobby Rhodes is a born leader, but he can never win. He knows exactly what must be done in a time of crisis, and he has the drive and imperative to make it happen, but he knows it won't work. And as he marches us, his loyal followers, toward certain destruction, we know it is righteous. As long as Bobby, our pimp, our fitness instructor, our patriarch, is calling the shots, the demons will not win. And yet, for Bobby to lead, he must also die. In *Demons 2,* Bobby is dragged down to a bloody end by the groin, even demons aware of the power of his manhood. In both films, Rhodes is a testament to the power and potential of a masochistic masculinity, smashing everything in sight to pave the way for salvation, finally allowing the self to be torn apart in a final rejection of one's inner demons.

THINKING HORROR:
An Exchange with s. j. bagley

Alex Houstoun

Despite the direct name, *THINKING HORROR: A Journal of Horror Philosophy* (https://thinkinghorrorjournal.wordpress.com/), defies a direct, simple summary. Started in 2015 by s. j. bagley and Simon Strantzas, the journal has positioned itself at odds with the majority of its contemporaries. As they describe it on the Thinking Horror website: "We've noticed there are a lot of journals devoted to horror fiction, and a lot devoted to horror-related non-fiction, but the two things they don't seem to cover with any regularity is 'what' and 'why.' Why horror? What is horror? These are the big questions that consume us, and we wanted to do something about it."

While these big questions drive *Thinking Horror*, it is the unique commitment to tackling these questions and an approach to the material that involves pushing further than most publications and individuals are comfortable going that compelled me to reach out to s. j. bagley. What follows is a discussion conducted via email in which bagley elaborated on their attraction to these big questions and some of their artistic and critical beliefs as they pertain to *Thinking Horror*.

AH: I would like to start by asking you to elaborate on the general concept of *Thinking Horror* and your motivation for starting the journal. You write on the website that the "unofficial theme" is "Why Horror?," which seems like an incredibly deceptive question—there are too many ways to understand it. Is it meant to be asking why we are drawn to horror; repulsed by horror; why horror as a literary genre even exists; why is something even considered horror; or is it perhaps some sort of horrible amalgamation of all of these questions and more?

sjb: The motivation began as a relatively simple one—the desire to interrogate writers about their work in a philosophical manner that goes deeper (and steps to the side of) the traditional interviews with horror writers and to take the sort of conversations that Simon Strantzas (the co-founder and associate editor of *Thinking Horror*) have had throughout the years—conversations that explore 'horror' and 'meaning' through a wider lens of philosophical criticism and, paradoxically i suppose, a very narrow take on personal meaning.

For a few years, i was coming up with titles for essays that didn't exist and posting them in various places on the Internet to spark discussion, and i had a pretty strong desire to start interviewing folks and, one day, Simon suggested combining the two (only with real essays by actual writers). i sat with the idea for a bit, bounced it off a few writers and critical readers, and eventually realized that it was something i felt necessary (especially given how so many interviews left me so frustrated with how shallow they were and the only places i could find good critical essays on horror were *Nightmare Magazine* and *Wormwood* and, while both tend to publish very quality work, i find each to have too narrow a focus to really scratch the itch).

As to 'why horror?' it's a matter of how simultaneously simple and complex the question is—some writers find it absolutely maddening and can go on for ages, while others can respond with a single sentence. i see it as a way to begin distinguishing between the real and the Real, philosophically, right out of the gate, and i steadfastly refuse to clarify the question if a writer asks for clarification—it's a fundamentally different question for each individual asked (and it did honestly give at least one of the interview subjects nightmares).

AH: There is a list of titles, available on the website for contributors to consider as an alternative to pitching an original essay: "Beyond the Past and the Past Beyond: The Intersection and Overlap of the Spectral and the Weird in Fritz Leiber's *Our Lady of Darkness,*" "All the Dark You Can Stand: Nyctophobia and Nyctophilia in the Work of Laird Barron," "Blood Splattered Black Denim: Examining the Liminal Between the Contemporary Literatures of Crime and Horror," to name a few. Is it reasonable to conclude that these titles are a continuation of your naming unwritten essays?

This may not be the right way to phrase it, but I am curious how you view the relationship of questions and answers; rather, the dynamic between the one who asks the question and the one who has to answer. If you are coming up with these titles, I would think it is fair to infer that you have a sense of how you might anticipate the nonexistent essay to unfold. However, in presenting these titles and subjects to the public without an essay attached you appear to be rejecting your own unwritten beliefs in the hope that someone will volunteer his or her beliefs instead. And yet, because you are the one asking the questions, interrogating the writer, you are control of the situation to a degree. I may be overdramatizing the editor-author dynamic . . .

sjb: Simon was canny enough to archive many of my essay titles, and those on the website are a handful of them. i tend to see them as i do most of my visual and sound art—once they're in the world, they no longer belong to me and, honestly, i relish the idea of someone actually using them to write an essay as i suspect that the dialectic relationship between my idea and their resulting work would lead to some very fertile ground. When you say 'However, in presenting these titles and subjects to the public without an essay attached you appear to be rejecting your own unwritten beliefs in hopes that someone will volunteer his or her's instead,' i see that as a more succinct way than i could put it. my idea/title must necessarily be functionally difficult from the writer's end result (especially since i steadfastly refuse to clarify the titles i come up with for those exercises).

As to the writer/interrogator dynamic, i see it as my duty to challenge writers in regard to their own work, even to the point of explaining to them, at times, that they're entirely wrong about an aspect of it, which then leads to a deeper layer of synthesis and a richer understanding of both the intent behind the work and the result of the work, which are often, and ideally, in a state of conflict. What the writer 'means' is never what the work 'means,' even though the two can sometimes be very close. i feel i should also mention that i reject the term 'author' for writers, as i see the actual authorship of a work to be what results from the dialectic between the writer (as effector) and the reader (as receptor). Somewhere in that nebulous middle ground lay the multiple 'truths' of the work.

i suppose i should admit there's a necessary sort of confrontational aspect to my interviewing style as i'm far more interested in challenging writers to discover something truly new about them and their work and to reject the premise of 'interview = promotional piece' that is far too common in the field. i'm far more interested in giving writers as much rope as they can take and watching the knots they tie in it (and, to be fair, occasionally, that knot can take the shape of a hangman's noose).

AH: Given that you confess to taking a "sort of" confrontational approach in your interviewing, I hope you'll permit me to push you a little bit right now. As a set-up, I agree completely with you that there is a disconnect between what a writer is trying to express and mean compared to what the resulting work may convey. Writing is generally a frustrating effort in which we are consistently failing to completely relate our thoughts; words are, among so many other things, rather limiting and awful.

Would you discuss your approach to writing? In particular, your choice to not capitalize "i" and how you view, and employ, parentheses. To call these acts a "stylistic choice" seems incredibly condescending, because there seems to be greater thought behind the actions and I believe, despite what I wrote earlier about the disconnect between a writer's intention and the end result, that there is a lot to be learned from one's very fundamental approach to words and writing.

sjb: Largely, my use of parenthesis (often layered) comes down to an intersection of the mathematical structure of language with the aesthetics of it—each sentence and phrase being structured as an equation within a larger whole which, for me, allows both an aesthetic unity of affect and a certain precision (which is perhaps a bit funny considering how much i value the expansive use of language in the work of others like Kiernan and Céline).

As to 'i,' it's a willful attempt to dismiss the idea of 'the self' as both participant and observer, allowing more important conceptual objects to come to fore and taking Derrida's 'il n'y a pas de horstexte' to a greater degree where there is not only no 'outside the text' but no 'self within the text' and fully embracing the concept of différance in a manner that distances 'my viewpoint' within the text from the observation of it.

AH: With regard to "mathematical structure of language" and its aesthetics, I wonder how this may influence your editing or composing and compiling an issue. Is the concept or theme of the issue what guides you in determining the arrangement, or do you react individually to the structure of each piece and try and create something in response?

sjb: Rigidly structuring *Thinking Horror* is something i've had to struggle against since i first started the journal, to be honest (especially since my publishing background is with almost ridiculously structured zines), and i mostly look to trying to make the arrangement accessible to the average reader by staggering interviews and essays.

That being said, i do take quite a bit of care in thinking about what begins and ends each volume and try to have the final piece be something that works as a coda to the entirety of it.

AH: You referred to creating art in other media. Do you consider *Thinking Horror* a body of art? Is your relationship with each issue, or the general concept of the journal, similar to what you described—a work that initially belongs to you but, once released upon the world, you surrender control? Further, to ask one of the most obnoxious questions possible, what do you perceive as art? Is the turning over of the work to the world necessary in determining if art has been made?

sjb: In the end, i see *Thinking Horror* as distinct from any body of art and, while i certainly see the interviews as collaborative, i try as much as i can to distance myself from the work contained within, seeing myself more as a curator than creator.

As to 'what is art,' i generally see it as a matter of 'art is context, not content,' with a widely variable concept of 'the gallery' (with the understanding that the art world and the gallery system are massively problematic, with deep-rooted problems in regard to race, class, gender, sexuality, accessibility). Art, for me, is absent the idea of 'beauty' and entirely focused around the idea of presentation and examination.

i should also state that i try to interfere with the essayists as little as possible, allowing them to express their own vision without too much in the way of guidance from me as, ultimately, the work is theirs and shouldn't reflect my own viewpoints, tastes, and politics.

AH: The first issue of *Thinking Horror* is centered, or curated, around the theme of "Horror in the Twenty-First Century" and issue two focuses on "The Horror Boom 1970–1992." Given that issue two has just been released—or will be released at the time that these words are being read—can you elaborate on the chosen subject? What is your relationship, if any, to the time period explored?

sjb: The idea to theme the second volume around the 'horror boom' came from Simon (it's a period that he has a great deal of interest in, and his idea that it's something that hasn't been properly explored with any depth is something i agree with).

My own connection to that period in horror is something akin to what most readers my age have—growing up with an abundance of horror literature that ranges in quality and thematic variety, from the sublime elegance of Steve Rasnic Tem's *Excavation* to the elegiac dreamscapes of Charles L. Grant's 'Oxrun' series to Poppy Z. Brite's early works of poetic cruelty to the highs and lows of the Splatterpunks and the nadir of the form that publishers like Zebra and Leisure churned out by the ton. It was a period where some of the most obscure and strange horror literature was able to find shelf space next to the most recent hackneyed work of empty bestsellers like John Saul. It was, to misquote Dickens, the best of times and the worst of times (and, often, it was difficult to know which end of the pool you were diving into with each new novel, anthology, collection, or story).

AH: You have mentioned Simon a few times now both as a co-founder of *Thinking Horror* and a general collaborator. I feel like a bit of a heel for not asking it sooner, or acknowledging the relationship described, but how do the two of you work together when it comes to *Thinking Horror*?

sjb: Aside from being the person who finally made me go forward with starting the damn thing, he has functioned in an advisory capacity and has been an essential resource for hashing out ideas with. Since the first volume, he has stepped back a bit to focus more on his writing, but i still see him as essential to the process of *Thinking Horror* (even when it simply comes down to me sending him a message at 3 A.M. to ask how he feels about something that is either brilliant or ridiculous and, for whatever reason, i can't determine which it is).

AH: Returning to your prior answer—my apologies for having adopted this habit of asking one new question and then having you back up to a previous answer—you mention your age in connection to the "Horror Boom," that the timing seemed to have worked out just right. What was it that first attracted you to the horror genre aside from the abundance of material available? Was there a deeper interest in the notion of horror, of being afraid, or were you captivated by the cover art? (Asking as one with very fond, very clear memories of browsing the books in the grocery store as a child looking for covers that disturbed me and similarly walking the horror aisle at Blockbuster.)

sjb: i had a very strange and largely awful childhood, and the combination of lifelong deep anxiety and early trauma drew me, from a very early age, to wanting to read suffering narratives and confessional works, and good horror can examine human suffering (physical and psychic) in a way that no other branch of literature really can. Works like Ketchum's *The Girl Next Door,* Barker's *Books of Blood,* and the aforementioned *Excavation* helped me process my own trauma and understand how trauma and personal horror can both effect and affect the landscapes of personality and society. In a very real way, horror literature (and horroresque literature like Beckett, Hamsun, Céline, and Acker) kept me alive when i was young and shaped a good deal about how i see and interact with the world around me. Hell, Barker's work was essential in my understanding what it meant to be queer, as a child, and i still recall how Brite's *Exquisite Corpse* helped me understand my own burgeoning views regarding gender (both my own and the entirety of the social construct),

It may seem counterintuitive, but my early immersion in horror literature and philosophy had far more to do with survival than pleasure (although i am far from the only person who was saved by monsters as a child). Eventually, the pleasure of aesthetics and thought became a massive part of it, but not until i was really able to process much of the trauma i experienced as a child.

AH: This draw to "the pleasure of aesthetics and thought" seems to go back to the initial question, "why horror?" although the pleasure was not the initial attraction . . .

You note that your turning to horror happens at an ideal time for the genre as "some of the most obscure and strange horror literature" was gaining equal exposure on the shelf with some really mediocre, forgettable works. It is wild to think that these kind of world-shattering or defining revelations would occur because you happened to pick the "right" book without much knowledge. I am old enough that I was exposed to some things by chance and good fortune—my musical development can be traced directly to a single mail-order slip from a punk label—but I am also young enough that I had the Internet as a shortcut during some fundamental years. I had the luxury of saying "I am feeling X today" or "I like this band, so what else is like this?" and then I could search around online and find strange little communities of people who felt the same. To borrow your analogy, there wasn't the same sense of diving into a pool and not knowing how deep it really was; you could do a little bit of gauging.

There were two questions I wanted to ask, and they have kind of become muddled into one: where do you generally see the horror genre or field now and simultaneously, how have things changed—or have they—from when you had to take a risk each time you picked a book off the shelf not knowing what quality of work it may hold? Regardless of the quality of writing in general, does the Internet and this ability to connect so easily with like-minded individuals—what are the odds that we would be emailing ten, fifteen years ago, let alone pre-2000?—foster a community, or is there something detrimental at work? I think, in particular, of your comment about wanting to challenge authors in interviews because the norm seems to be to accept and praise those with a vague common interest. This is more than two questions, sorry.

sjb: The Internet has been the worst and best thing ever created, and i think that weird dichotomy is perfectly on display when it comes to horror writers/readers and the idea of 'community.' It has allowed terrible writers to publish with no fear of failure while allowing wonderful writers to publish with no fear of success. It's allowed for more participatory conversation and analysis, but equally allows for the ignoring of anything like decent criticism. It's a simultaneous echo chamber and vacuum chamber, and we've only begun to explore its possibilities.

In many ways, i'm pretty happy to have started my experiences with horror literature (as well as music and art) before the birth of the World Wide Web, but i certainly don't miss having to get tapes in the mail from England just to hear what new jams John Peel was spinning or having to buy badly photocopied zines (pirated by ten different people by the time they get to me) just to finally read a Ligotti story.

In the end, i think that a certain sense of isolation was important for my development as a person, philosopher, and critic, and i think that having that background has made me more able to take a step back from everything, every now and again, and look at it all with a fresh set of eyes and expectations, but i don't begrudge younger folks having the access that they do and i think that access has led to two fundamental changes in regard to the creation of horror literature: 1) the small press has become an incredibly fecund area with some of the best horror literature of the last century appearing from publishers like Undertow and Word Horde (which, of course, has its flipside in the fact that so much of the small press is just poorly produced garbage, but a collection as stunning as Eric Schaller's *Meet Me in the Middle of the Air* simply couldn't be published by a major New York publisher), and 2) it's allowed for the psychic landscape of horror to shift to something more internal than what we largely saw in the '70s–'90s, exploring things like anxiety, depression, and the idea of disintegrating selfhood in ways that simply couldn't have worked during the boom period (where most of the work was focused on very conservative social ideas).

As to wanting to challenge writers, that's another area where the Internet is as terrible as it is wonderful—it allows a democratization of contact between writers and readers. It allows terrible writers to feel as if they're 'successful' because they can surround themselves with fans on Facebook, and it allows good writers to wallow in despair and self-doubt due to how difficult it can be to really trust fans. So going back to how i try to challenge writers—i intentionally step away from the toxic morass of 'fandom' and try to force the writers into a deeper understanding of *what* they are writing and not just *why* they are writing. So far, most of the writers i've tried to interview have found the process rather grueling, but they've appreciated (there have been a few failures where they simply weren't able to get away from the idea of an interview being specifically for promotional purposes or simply couldn't dig as deep enough as i wanted them to).

AH: This conflict between the *what* and *why* of writing was something I wanted to ask you about, but you have also brought up another point that I wanted to raise, so I am going to meld them together and really hope for the best: the horror boom was largely fueled, and popularized, by a very socially conservative sort of horror, whereas the genre has now moved primarily to something more abstract and leftist—to highlight the difference from the old. "Leftist" is not the right way to put it, because that implies simply politics, and I mean to include that there also now seems to be a greater effort to engage critically with writers and their work, to analyze and deconstruct. There seems to be—and this really could be simply an Internet echo chamber—a push to engage as readers and writers in a more proactive and critical manner. If the Internet has allowed readers and writers to connect directly, it has also allowed aspiring intellectuals and critics to do so as well and inject a new type of discourse into the discussion.

I think this development is somewhat entwined with people moving from a *why* mentality—I am writing this because I am upset with the changes unfolding around me and I am reacting against them—to *what:* I am writing and reading to explore a situation or a sensation not just because I am upset or disturbed but because I can use it as a vessel to push further an idea.

First, do you think there are any limitations in this wide opening of the sort of horror writing that is now published? If things like "anxiety, depression, and the idea of disintegrating selfhood" might not have worked during the boom period, are there aspects of horror that are currently at a disadvantage? More so, is that actually an issue (especially if all we are experiencing is a dearth of socially conservative horror stories)?

If the focus shifts from the *why* to the *what* becomes more normalized and the sort of interrogative interview you engage in becomes less alien to authors, do you see *Thinking Horror* evolving further or is the function it is currently serving adequate? You have made it quite clear that *Thinking Horror* is meant to push writers both in the work they submit and in submitting to your interviews and in doing so it also pushes the readers—it is not a journal to be taken lightly. Does that mean it has to continue to evolve or, as a project, if it becomes more normalized do you see yourself moving on to something new?

sjb: i do think there are built-in limitations to the opening/widening of experience within horror literature, but i'm not convinced of just what those limitations are. As to whether there are aspects of horror that are currently at a disadvantage—absolutely. Death is a good example—the cutting edge of contemporary horror is less concerned with 'death' as both object and endpoint and more concerned with what surrounds 'death,' both psychically and culturally. We see more successful (both in terms of literary quality and the market) work that deals more with survival and what happens *after* trauma, while work that focuses on the idea of the protagonist being in mortal danger has shifted away from horror (while still being popular in the thriller (but, even there, its popularity seems on the decline).

Thinking Horror is an organism that i see in constant evolution, with no real end point in sight. What i want from it, what it really means, is in a state of constant flux that simultaneously produces forward momentum and a hell of a lot of personal anxiety. i do honestly hope that readers come away from it understanding that they can and should demand more from writers, and i hope that writers come away from it understanding that they'll produce better work by challenging themselves and the expectations of the reading public. Literary history has long shown that challenging literature can stand the test of time far better than work in which the writer simply plays it safe. i mean, hell, the main reason Lovecraft is still argued about so much today is that his work is far more challenging (aesthetically, philosophically, and politically) than the temporally more successful Seabury Quinn, who is now barely remembered at all. One only needs to look to the fact that Shirley Jackson's work is experiencing a resurgence to see that horror literature that challenges us and makes us better readers for having experienced it can stand the test of time.

As to the future of the project, i do think it will have to continue to change in order to remain relevant and the very moment that i feel it's achieved all it can, i will walk away, turn off the lights, and move on to something new. That being said, i do feel the project has a least few years of life left in it!

AH: Speaking of the future, the first two issues of *Thinking Horror* are currently available. Can we expect the third within a year, as that seems to be the release schedule? Do you have a theme in mind for the next issue or is it too soon to ask?

sjb: The third volume will be themed around 'religion, spirituality, and the occult in horror' (with as broad a definition of those things as can be imagined) and will (hopefully!) be out in the third quarter of 2018.

AH: Are there any other projects that you are working on that are available to readers? Are you still making zines? How can one learn more about your sound and visual art?

sjb: My sound art can largely be found on my bandcamp (heksenhaus.bandcamp.com), while much of my visual work can be found on tumblr (heksenhaus.tumblr.com). And as for other projects—i'm slowly working on a editing a critical examination of the work of Jeffrey Thomas, a critical edition of Lovecraft's "The Colour out of Space," and an anthology of New England folk horror stories (the last of which should be out this summer from the good folks of Orford Parish Books). In the years to come, i plan to edit a few more fiction anthologies, more critical works, and maybe an anthology of avant garde/abstract comics as well as continuing the visual and sound work.

AH: To close out. . . you read anything good lately?

sjb: i've been obsessively reading all the comics i can find by Michael Deforge and Mickey Z. (her *RAV* might be the best science fiction comic since *Akira*), and i've been lucky enough to spend some time with some truly great debut collections from Christopher Slatsky, Jon Padgett, and Sunny Morraine, new work from Caitlín R. Kiernan, Ray Cluley, and Matthew M. Bartlett, contemporary philosophy work by Robin James and Katereina Kolozova, anonymous trans narratives, and every one of the lovely little chapbooks that Dim Shores releases. i also tend to do one big reading project per year and this year i'm rereading all the collected short fiction by Joyce Carol Oates (with the hope of maybe editing a critical volume about her work, at some point).

Pastiches of Pastiches
S. T. Joshi

BRIAN M. SAMMONS and GLYNN OWEN BARRASS, ed. *The Children of Gla'aki: A Tribute to Ramsey Campbell's Great Old One*. Portland, OR: Dark Regions Press, 2017. 292 pp. ISBN: 978-1-62641-194-4. $20.00 tpb. (A signed/limited hc has been announced at $150.00.)

On the face of it, the prospect of an entire volume of stories that imitate the Lovecraftian imitations of a British teenager would not be very appealing. Are there really people out there who want to read pastiches of pastiches? Apparently there are, but even those who think there is some merit or enjoyment in such writing are bound to be disappointed by the farrago of uninspired conceptions and sheer bad writing that pollutes this volume from beginning to end.

The most interesting thing about this book is its subtitle. What it purports to be is a tribute, not to Campbell himself, but specifically to his imaginary god Gla'aki (formerly known as Glaaki—Campbell has made a point of adding the glottal stop in his recent work). It is of course hopeless for any contemporary writers—excepting, perhaps, Caitlín R. Kiernan, Thomas Ligotti, and Jonathan Thomas—to write stories modelled upon the revolutionary work that Campbell began writing after he left behind the adolescent Lovecraftian tales entombed in *The Inhabitant of the Lake and Less Welcome Tenants* (Arkham House, 1964). It is this work—beginning with *Demons by Daylight* (Arkham House, 1973) and continuing on through dozens of other novels, novellas, and short story collections—that has given Campbell an unassailable place in contemporary weird fiction. As such, *The Children of Gla'aki* stands in stark contrast to Scott David Aniolowski's *Made in Goatswood: A Celebration of Ramsey Campbell* (Chaosium, 1995). It cannot be said that that latter volume focused much beyond Campbell's Lovecraftian tales, but it had a much more impressive lineup of contributors (among them A. A. Attanasio, Richard A. Lupoff, Peter Cannon, and several other notables) than *Children of Gla'aki* and, accordingly, a substantially higher level of quality.

What this book offers is a rather monotonous emphasis on the god Gla'aki, trapped in a lake in Brichester (he had come down on a meteor that had landed there, creating the lake), or appearances of Gla'aki in other bodies of water around the world. Campbell's own story "The Inhabitant of the Lake" leads off the volume—an unfortunate choice in itself, because this weak imitation of Lovecraft's "The Whisperer in Darkness" is by no means the best of the *Inhabitant* tales, or even the best of the Lovecraftian tales that Campbell had written around that time.[1]

Some authors make exactly the same mistake that Campbell did in writing his own Lovecraftian pastiches. Just as Campbell wrote several tales set in the New England of the 1920s—a realm he knew little about—so do some of the writers in *Gla'aki* set their stories in a British milieu, or in the 1920s, or both. Nick Mamatas's lackluster "Country Mouse, City Mouse" tells of a pair of twins from Cyprus, one of whom goes to the Severn Valley and finds himself in the "city of Gla'aki." The story does little more than showcase the author's

---

1. See the augmented edition, *The Inhabitant of the Lake and Other Unwelcome Tenants* (PS Publishing, 2011),which contains other Lovecraftian stories not included in the original *Inhabitant* volume.

superficial knowledge (easily acquired via the Internet) of contemporary British culture and lingo. Josh Reynolds's "Squatters [*sic*] Rights" is set in 1921 and introduces us to Charles St. Cyprian, who it transpires holds the post of Royal Occultist—a position originating with John Dee from Queen Elizabeth I's reign. When a corpse horribly afflicted with the "green decay" (a detail cited in Campbell's "Inhabitant of the Lake") is found in the flat of one Philip Wendy-Smythe, who has purchased the series of houses at Lakewood [*sic*] Terrace near where Gla'aki resides, St. Cyprian seeks to return the deed of purchase to the real estate agent who sold the property to Wendy-Smythe. Aside from being so remarkably ahead of his time as to refer to one character as "Ms. Gallowglass," St. Cyprian has to battle an army of reanimated corpses who besiege him on all sides. One can charitably assume this story was meant as a parody.

Robert M. Price ("In Search of Lake Monsters"), never one to say no to writing sterile imitations, introduces us to one Langdon Rivenbark, a professor at Brichester University who grudgingly participates in a documentary film about sightings of Gla'aki in the lake. Predictably, the divers who plunge into the lake send back footage of strange sea creatures and other odd phenomena. But Price undercuts his own story by ludicrously describing Gla'aki as "a kind of glistening rubbery potato."

A television show, *Haunted: Dead or Alive,* is the focus of Tim Curran's "Night of the Hopfrog." Here we are again taken to Lakeside Terrace in Brichester, where two teams of ghost-hunters explore one of the houses near the shore and again encounter peculiar and horrible creatures. Curran indulges in an orgy of all-capitals in a bootless attempt to convey a sense of oh-my-god horror to the reader.

William Meikle is very clearly an author with nothing of his own to say, as he has attempted to make a career by writing pastiches of William Hope Hodgson's Carnacki stories—which themselves were spinoffs of Algernon Blackwood's John Silence stories. Whereas Blackwood's tales show considerable depth of conception and vividness of imagery, Hodgson's show very little; and Meikle's show even less. In "The Lakeside Cottages" Meikle actually has Carnacki battle Gla'aki, using the same kind of occultist mumbo-jumbo (the "Saamaaa Ritual" and so forth) that makes Hodgson's Carnacki stories so preposterous. After reading this story, I am deeply perplexed at the very reason for Meikle's existence as a writer.

Another individual whose permanent retirement from the realm of authorship can only be a benefit to the human race is Edward Morris. In "I Want to Break Free" Morris begins with a ham-fisted pastiche of Lovecraft's "The Colour out of Space," then proceeds to a moony treatment of a man in Brichester who falls under the sway of Gla'aki. This volume reaches its nadir with Pete Rawlik's "The Collection of Gibson Flynn," in which a rabid book collector in Florida will do just about anything to gain possession of a volume of *The Revelations of Gla'aki* once owned by Errol Undercliffe (a character in some of Campbell's *Demons by Daylight* stories). Let it pass that Rawlik gets a number of details wrong about the rare books he is discussing: we are introduced to *Azathoth and Others* by Edward Pickman Derby (Lovecraft, in "The Thing on the Doorstep," refers to the book as *Azathoth and Other Horrors*); and when he cites Zorad Ethan Hoag's *Dreams from R'lyeh,* Rawlik seems entirely unaware that this was an actual book of poetry by Lin Carter published by Arkham House in 1975. But these blemishes are only the tip of the iceberg of Rawlik's derelictions, for the tale quickly descends to an orgy of pornographic sadism and scatology that serves no aesthetic purpose.

In Scott R. Jones's story "The Spike," a character ridiculously named Domitian Hark begins work for a company whose CEO is Aldo Tusk—an obvious riff on Elon Musk, although it is unclear whether the resemblances between the real and the fictional character extend to much beyond the name. In any event, it turns out that Tusk's remarkable discoveries (including, incidentally, a cure for cancer) were the result of material derived from the spikes that Gla'aki habitually sports on his person. The plot of Jones's story is of some minimal interest, but it is spoiled by a prose style that fluctuates wildly from the slipshod to the ponderous. For you see, Jones is very fond of sentence fragments. Very dramatic. Something like this. Get the picture?

In Lee Clarke Zumpe's "Beneath Cayuga's Churning Waves" we are interested to learn that Gla'aki is now in one of the Finger Lakes in upstate New York, as a determined investigative reporter, Tisha Hewitt, learns to her peril. Orrin Grey's "Invaders of Gla'aki" tells of a video game based on Gla'aki to which one teenage boy becomes addicted. This tale has some poignancy and terror, but it needs further development. Tom Lynch's "Scion of Chaahk" finds Gla'aki near the ruins of Chichén Itzá in the Yucatán; how he ever got there is a mystery. Thana Niveau's "The Dawning of His Dreams" is an effective but not entirely coherent prose-poem about Gla'aki and some unspecified "aliens" whom he has subjugated. And I scarcely know what to make of Kostantine Paradias's "Cult of Panacea," a perfectly incomprehensible horror/science fiction tale about Gla'aki.

Only a few stories in this book have any merits at all. W. H. Pugmire ("The Secret Painting of Thomas Cartwright") can always be relied on to provide his patented conglomeration of exquisite prose-poetry, profound Lovecraftian (and, in this case, Campbellian) sensitivity, and delicacy of character portrayal. Here Gla'aki—or, rather, an "aspect of its eidolon"—is found in Sesqua Valley, Pugmire's evocative Pacific Northwest parallel to Lovecraft's haunted New England and Campbell's mysterious Severn Valley.

John Goodrich's "Tribute Band" speaks of the baleful results that follow when the member of a band, Murderous Dwarfs—a "tribute band" to the Goatswood Gnomes of decades past—comes upon the ninth volume of *The Revelations of Gla'aki* and becomes obsessed with it. It appears that the leader of the Goatswood Gnomes, Brian Brady, has been trapped in a "plane of sound"—an ingenious reference to Campbell's early and innovative story "The Plain of Sound," one of several tales in *The Inhabitant of the Lake* that showed traces of the originality and dynamism that he would soon be displaying in his later work. I will excuse the fact that Goodrich has written "You broached [he means 'breached'] the walls of sound, and now Gla'aki is free."

Tim Waggoner's "Nature of Water" is the affecting tale of a man, Mark, who as a twelve-year-old boy had taken up with a slightly younger boy, Dustin, at Lake Clearshore (in an unspecified area of the United States). Irritated at Dustin's smart-aleck ways, Mark had dumped Dustin into the lake, whereupon he had disappeared. From that point on, Mark's life is marred by alcoholism, failed relationships, and a general sense of futility. Now, at age forty-two, Mark encounters Dustin's ghost—who, in a plangent parody of an Alcoholics Anonymous slogan, urges Mark to seek "the help of a higher power." This tale shows how weird fiction can be used to convey profound emotions and shed light on human frailties. John Langan's "Mirror Fishing" begins as a light-hearted fantasy wherein nineteen-year-old Lisa, babysitting her teenage cousin Patrick, leads him bodily through a mirror to encounter what in old Scots legend is called Auld Glaikit. But the tale quickly takes a darker turn, leading to grisly death and horror.

Aside from these few stories, *The Children of Gla'aki* is a hopeless mess. And the saddest piece in the book is Campbell's own afterword, where he is forced to say polite things about the wretched stories that were ostensibly designed as a tribute to him but prove to be unwitting parodies of his early writing. As I have suggested, this volume was misguided in its very conception, and the resulting array of mediocrity—occasionally descending to actively offensive dreadfulness—was only to be expected.

About the Contributors

Michael J. Abolafia is an editor, writer, and archivist with a B.A. in English from Columbia University. He co-edited, for Hippocampus Press, a critical edition of David Park Barnitz's *The Book of Jade* and has contributed essays and articles to *Lovecraft Annual, Spectral Realms,* the *New York Daily News, Brooklyn Magazine, Supernatural Tales,* and other periodicals. He will begin studying for an M.St. in English (1900–present) at the University of Oxford in Fall 2017, where he plans to write a thesis on the Auden Generation using new archival materials he uncovered.

Gavin Callaghan's work has appeared in *Studies in Weird Fiction, Lovecraft Annual,* the *Comics Journal, Wormwood, FATE* magazine, and *The Book of Jade: A New Critical Edition*. He hails from New York's Southern Tier.

Ramsey Campbell is an English horror fiction writer, editor, and critic who has been writing for well over fifty years. He is frequently cited as one of the leading writers in the field.

Nathan Chazan is from Toronto. His writing has previously appeared in *Cleaver Magazine* and the *Cornell Daily Sun*.

Jose Cruz is an author based in southwest Florida whose work is forthcoming or has previously appeared in *Rue Morgue, Nightscript, Turn to Ash, bare•bones* e-zine, and the *Year's Best Hardcore Horror Stories*.

Taij Devon was born in New Delhi and grew up in State College, Pennsylvania. After graduating from Vassar College, he joined the Marines. He currently resides in Baton Rouge.

Amber Doll Diaz is a South Bronx native whose poetry and film reviews have been featured in the *Northern Valley Suburbanite* and the *Cosmicomicon*. She lives in Englewood, New Jersey, with her two cats.

Ashley Dioses is a poet of dark fantasy and horror from Southern California. Her debut poetry collection, *Diary of a Sorceress,* is forthcoming from Hippocampus Press in 2018.

Stephanie Graves is an instructor at the University of North Alabama and is currently pursuing her Ph.D. in English at Georgia State University. Her research interests include horror, the grotesque, and the Southern Gothic.

Alex Houstoun is a co-editor of *Dead Reckonings*.

S. T. Joshi is the author of such critical and biographical studies as *The Weird Tale* (1990), *I Am Providence: The Life and Times of H. P. Lovecraft* (2010), and *Unutterable Horror: A History of Supernatural Fiction* (2012). He has prepared corrected editions of H. P. Lovecraft's work for Arkham House and annotated editions of the weird tales of Lovecraft, Algernon Blackwood, Lord Dunsany, M. R. James, Arthur Machen, and Clark Ashton Smith for Penguin Classics, as well as the anthology *American Supernatural Tales* (2007).

Alexander Lugo studies English and Classics at Cornell University.

James Machin is a London-based scholar with an interest in early weird fiction, among other things. He is the co-editor of *Faunus,* the journal of the Friends of Arthur Machen.

Daniel Pietersen is a writer of weird fiction and horror philosophy. Recent publications include a piece of weird short fiction in the *Audient Void* and an essay on the nature of horror in Clive Barker's "The Hellbound Heart," for the second volume of *Thinking Horror*. He has a blog of fragmentary work and other thoughts at https://constantuniversity.wordpress.com/.

Darrell Schweitzer is an American writer, editor, and critic in the field of speculative fiction. Much of his focus has been on dark fantasy and horror, although he also does work in science fiction and fantasy. His latest book is *The Threshold of Forever: Essays and Reviews*.

Bev Vincent is best known as the author of *The Road to the Dark Tower,* the Bram Stoker Award–nominated authorized companion to Stephen King's *Dark Tower* series, and *The Stephen King Illustrated Companion*, which was nominated for a 2010 Edgar Award.

Hank Wagner is a respected critic and journalist. Among the many publications in which his work regularly appears are *Cemetery Dance* and *Mystery Scene*.

www.ingramcontent.com/pod-product-compliance
Lightning Source LLC
Chambersburg PA
CBHW061752020426
42331CB00006B/1442